The
Kodály Method II
Folksong to Masterwork

LOIS CHOKSY

The University of Calgary

Prentice Hall, Upper Saddle River, New Jersey 07458

Library of Congress Cataloging-in-Publication Data

CHOKSY, LOIS.
   The Kodály method II: folksong to masterwork / Lois Choksy.
     p. cm.
   Includes bibliographical references (p.), discography (p.),
  and index.
   ISBN 0-13-949173-2
   1. Music—Instruction and study. 2. Music appreciation.
  3. Kodály, Zoltán, 1882–1967. I. Title.
  MT1.C5366   1999
  372.87—dc21   98-10892

Editorial director: *Charlyce Jones Owen*
Acquisitions editor: *Bud Therien*
Production editor: *Edie Riker*
Cover director: *Jayne Conte*
Cover design: *Bruce Kenselaar*
Cover photo: *Lois Choksy*
Buyer: *Bob Anderson*
Marketing manager: *Sheryl Adams*
Editorial assistant: *Mary Amoon*
Frontispiece: sculpture by *Dora de Pédery-Hunt* / photo by *Elizabeth Frey*

This book was set in 10/12 Times Roman by Preparé/Emilcomp
and it was printed and bound by Courier Companies, Inc.
The cover was printed by Phoenix Color Corp.

© 1999 by Prentice-Hall, Inc.
A Pearson Education Company
Upper Saddle River, NJ 07458

Printed in the United States of America

10 9 8 7 6 5 4 3 2 1

ISBN 0-13-949173-2

Prentice-Hall International (UK) Limited,London
Prentice-Hall of Australia Pty. Limited, Sydney
Prentice-Hall Canada Inc., Toronto
Prentice-Hall Hispanoamericana, S.A., Mexico
Prentice-Hall of India Private Limited, New Delhi
Prentice-Hall of Japan, Inc., Tokyo
Pearson Education Asia Pte. Ltd., Singapore
Editora Prentice-Hall do Brasil, Ltda., Rio de Janeiro

Contents

Chapter 4

First Experiences in Directed Listening   82

Chapter 5

Experiences in Directed Listening:
The Symphony and Sonata Form   110

Chapter 6

Experiences in Directed Listening:
Music of the Baroque (1600–1750)   132

Preface

KODÁLY'S LEGACY

Zoltan Kodály's prolific writing has bequeathed to twentieth-century music education a philosophy so rich and all-encompassing that it is small wonder there is hardly a corner of the world to which it has not reached. There is Kodály practice today in every province in Canada, in most of the fifty states, in England, Australia and New Zealand, Belgium, France, Spain, Italy, Switzerland, Estonia, Poland, Denmark, Iceland, Finland, the Union of South Africa, Japan, and China. There are national Kodály Societies in many of these places.

It is not the superficial techniques associated with Kodály (the *ti-ta*'s, *solfa*, and hand-signs) that have caused this. These pedagogical techniques—while effective—all existed long before Kodály was born. England had had a system of movable-*do* and hand-signs in its music education for nearly one hundred years before Kodály first observed them in use there. *Solfa* itself is nearly a thousand years old, and hand-signs were used to lead Hebrew congregational singing before the birth of Christ.

Like the teaching techniques, the pedagogical process associated with Kodály contains nothing new. The principles of preparing for new learning over a period of time, of uncovering a new learning through a carefully guided discovery process and then reinforcing it through practice—this view of the educational process can be traced at least to Pestalozzi and probably even earlier—or, if one really wishes to look back in time, to the ancient Greeks who seemed to have understood very well what education should—at its best—be.

What is it then that so fires the imagination and causes the sure, steady expansion of Kodály practice worldwide? The answer may be found in Kodály's own words—in the speeches and lectures he gave and in the many articles he wrote. The simple eloquence with which he expressed the necessity of a comprehensive music education for all peoples speaks to an inner certainty in everyone who reads or hears his words:

...No man is complete without music.... general education must include music.

You cannot nourish a child if you give him something to eat only once a week.... music must be taken every day.

...not to make [of students] professional musicians—just to complete them as people.[1]

Techniques do not stir the imagination; *solfa* and *ti-ta*'s never set anybody on fire; pedagogical processes do not give excitement and purpose to life. Ideas do. The idea that through music and through the way we teach music we can significantly improve the quality of life:

Powerful sources of spiritual enrichment spring from music. We must spare no effort to have them opened for as many people as possible.[2]

The idea that everyone can know and enjoy music in a way that in past centuries only trained musicians could:

In 1690 [the] idea that everybody could learn to read and write their own language was at least as bold as the idea today that everybody should learn to read music. Nevertheless, it is something no less possible.

It is the right of every citizen to be taught the basic elements of music, to be handed the key with which he can enter the locked world of music.[3]

The idea that everyone can sing and through singing can become part of what Kodály called a *Universal Harmony*:

It is the richness of both the musical experiences themselves and the memory of them that makes a good musician. Individual singing plus listening to music... develops the ear to such an extent that one understands music one has heard with as much clarity as if one were looking at a score; if necessary—and if time permits—one should be able to reproduce such a score. This, and certainly no less, is what we expect from the student of a language; and music is a manifestation of the human spirit similar to a language.[4]

The idea that people can be led to better understand themselves and their surroundings if their first music is the music of their own peoples, history, and culture...; that a sense of roots, of belonging, can be imparted even to today's mobile, nomadic population through their heritage of folk songs:

---

[1] Interview with Ernö Daniel, Santa Barbara, August, 1966.

[2] Kodály, *Selected Writings*, p.120.

[3] Kodály, *Selected Writings*, pp.120 and 77.

[4] Kodály, *Selected Writings*, p. ???.

First of all, a good folk song is a perfect masterpiece in itself.

Only the music which has sprung from the ancient musical traditions of a people can reach the masses of that people.

...folksongs offer such a rich variety of moods and perspectives that the child grows in human consciousness, feeling more and more at home in his country.

...and the big classics—the great classics—are always, in the end, related somehow to the folk music of their composers' own country... Haydn to the Austrian, Beethoven to the German.[5]

The idea that music should be the core—the very heart of the curriculum—because:

Through music we possess a means for a general development of the human soul... a means that cannot be replaced by any other subject... the elements of music are precious instruments in education. Rhythm develops attention, concentration, determination, and the ability to condition oneself. Melody opens up the world of the emotions. Dynamic variation and tone colour sharpen our hearing. Singing... is such a many-sided physical activity that its effect in physical education is immeasurable.[6]

[We must] tackle the problem of providing musical education for the public.... Our aim must be to turn out children for whom music, good music, is a necessity of life.[7]

It is clear that what Kodály offers isn't a *method*—although method may be used to support it. It is, rather, a vision of what the world could be like if it were the property of musicians rather than politicians.

Lois Choksy
Professor of Music
The University of Calgary

---

[5] a), c), d): *Kodály and Education*, pp. 46, 62, 71; b): *Selected Writings*, p. 30.
[6] Kodály, *Selected Writings*, p. 130.
[7] Eósze, p. 74.

The
Kodály Method II

Chapter 1

Kodály in North America

The Kodály Approach has existed in North American music education programs for more than thirty years. It has permeated teaching behaviors and infiltrated classrooms to the point where it is doubtful that there is a school music lesson taught in which some vestige of Kodály practice—use of *solfa*, hand-signs, rhythm syllables, indigenous folk songs—may not be found. Occasionally, teachers utilizing these tools associated with the Kodály Method are not even aware of them as such. They are simply emulating others in their school districts, or, in the case of younger teachers, teaching as they were taught to teach.[1]

This is not a bad thing. For any approach to endure, it must enter the mainstream of music education. It cannot remain separate and apart. However, while many teachers now appear to be conversant with, and even knowledgeable about Kodály techniques for bringing musical knowledge and skills to five-, six-, seven-, and eight-year-olds, there is little evidence at the upper grade levels and in the secondary schools that teachers are building upon these children's musical knowledge and skill in a progressive way.

At the upper elementary grades students often simply get "more of the same." They sing more folk songs, they sing them in *solfa* and *ti-ta*'s, they become more facile with hand-signs, and sometimes they read music a bit more proficiently. They become more able at skills they already possess, but they do not generally add new skills; and rarely are they led to infer more advanced concepts or to acquire further musical knowledge.

At the middle school, junior high, or secondary school levels the picture is even bleaker. Since few secondary school teachers are fluent with the musical vocabulary familiar to their students from the elementary school—the *solfa* and *ti-ta*'s and hand-signs—these teachers tend to begin again, as if their students have no musical background on which to draw. There is frequent reference in the literature to the gap

---

[1] Increasing numbers of teacher-training programs are including Kodály principles and practice in their curricula.

between elementary and secondary school music education as something that must be bridged.

There is no gap. There is only the necessity for accessing what students know and moving forward step by step from that base.

Curriculum theory underlying music education at the upper elementary or secondary school level is not different from curriculum theory underlying music education at the preschool and primary grade levels. Curriculum cannot be constructed from the bottom up without first recognizing the desired end product, the final outcome teachers wish to see as a result of the educative process. It is essential to know with great surety that desired outcome. Once it is known it is possible to determine what instructional objectives are necessary and what learning strategies must be employed at each grade level to achieve that final goal.

DESIRED END PRODUCT

Any intelligently conceived curriculum must begin with a clear idea of what that end product is to be.

What should students be like at the end of twelve years of music education? What difference should music instruction have made, and continue to make in their lives? It might be useful to draw a profile of an "ideal" graduating twelfth-grade music student. For purposes of this exercise, the realities of insufficient time scheduled for music, inadequate facilities, crowded classrooms, overscheduled teachers and music taught by musically inadequate classroom teachers will be suspended. This imaginary student has had music at least twice weekly, taught by a competent music specialist, since kindergarten.

What, under ideal teaching circumstances, will the graduating twelfth-grade student possess musically?

First, he or she will love music. For this student, good music is not a frill or an entertainment, but a necessity of life. This will be evidenced for the rest of his or her life though concert attendance, purchase of high quality sound systems (perhaps even before a car), and an ongoing expenditure on recordings.

He or she will play in the community orchestra or sing in the opera chorus. Later in life, when financial circumstances permit, he or she will serve on the symphony board or perhaps even on one of the national committees that make decisions as to which young musicians should receive financial support in the form of grants or awards.

Perhaps of four hundred graduating twelfth graders in the district, this one may even choose to become a professional musician. One out of four hundred is enough. Knowledgeable audiences and a public ready to support music financially in the schools and community are needed in far greater numbers than are professional musicians.

But all of this is merely the most obvious and visible result of what a sound music education has done for this student. What is the musical knowledge and what are the musical skills possessed by this students that have led him or her to place such value on music?

This mythical student not only loves and supports music; he or she also:

- has achieved a high musical standard in performance.
- knowledgeably critiques performances, including his or her own, and makes or suggests desirable changes.
- has performed, listened to, and analysed a wide variety of musical literature from all periods and styles.
- has developed vocal independence and a high level of vocal sight reading proficiency. He or she can both look at notation and think sound, and think or hear sound and notate it correctly.
- uses technical vocabulary correctly in analysing and describing music.
- understands scientific principles of sound production and reproduction.
- understands the technical and theoretical aspects of music.
- is knowledgeable about the historical development of music.
- understands compositional techniques and is able on an amateur level to improvise and compose in a variety of styles.
- is able to discuss intelligently a variety of topics regarding music and musicians.[2]

In general, he or she has acquired knowledge, skills, and a highly sophisticated set of musical values and standards with which to support that "love of music" mentioned first. How can the teacher prepare this extraordinary student, especially while getting ready for the Music Festival, the Christmas Program, the Choral Competition, or the Spring Band Concert? The Music Festival, the Christmas Program, the Choral Competition, or the Spring Band Concert should not be viewed as goals. They are simply not deserving of that position in any curricular framework. Teachers must cease viewing these necessary activities as ends and start viewing them as means.

The teaching perspective must change from "I have these five pieces and I have to get the band (or choir) ready to perform them by April 12th," to "I have these five pieces the band (or choir) has to perform."

- *What can I teach about music through these pieces?*
- *From what historical period or style are they?*
- *What have we previously studied to which I can relate them?*
- *How can I make the musical reading of this material more proficient?*
- *What compositional devices are used with which the students are familiar? Are there new compositional techniques utilized that we should analyse?*
- *Are there opportunities in any of these pieces for students to experiment with improvisation or composition?*
- *How can I use these pieces to further students' music writing skills and to extend their understanding of harmony and theory?*
- *What musical decisions regarding their performance could the students themselves be involved in making?*

---

[2] Many of these outcomes are based on ones that originally appeared in *Creating Curriculum in Music*, Edelstein, Choksy, Lehman, Sigurdsson, and Woods (Addison-Wesley, 1980).

Teachers sometimes feel they haven't time for this kind of depth in band, choir, elementary vocal or junior high general music classes. To the contrary, there is insufficient time to teach in any other way.

In the long run, students who are more musically knowledgeable will be better performers. Time spent teaching music rather than preparing pieces is time well spent. The former has implications for life-long music making. The latter is forgotten a week after the concert. Performing well is a desirable outcome; but it is only one of many equally important outcomes of music education, and it is often the least effective goal over the long term. Five years after graduation, where are those students who were in band or choir throughout their secondary school years? What are they doing with their music? For most former band students, the clarinet is in the closet, where it has been for the past five years. Choir student post-graduate involvement in music is less well documented but there is little reason to suppose it is better. It seems apparent that a school music education program of which performance is the primary focus is simply missing the boat.

Returning to that mythical twelfth-grade grade student described earlier, what must the music teacher do to create this musically literate, knowledgeable, dedicated amateur? First it is necessary to broaden the focus. Performing, while admittedly important, is only one of four important basic musical behaviors:

- performing
- listening
- analyzing
- creating

Through **performing**, students:

- develop repertory
- work toward good ensemble and solo sound
- master technical aspects of playing and singing

Through **listening**, students:

- acquire knowledge of the great music literature
- become familiar with many periods, styles, and genres; develop a sense of style and period
- develop historic perspective
- discover what the artist brings to the music; performance practice
- analyze compositional techniques

Through **analyzing**, students develop the skills necessary for intelligent performance and listening, including:

- musical reading
- musical writing

- study of intervals, scales, modes, and harmony
- derivation of musical forms
- development of inner hearing skills

Through **creating**, students:

- come to better understand the compositional techniques and devices of the music they perform, listen to, and analyze
- use the materials of music to organize their own productions either improvised or composed
- synthesize all other musical learning

Any one of these four musical behaviors may be the focus of any lesson, or indeed the primary focus of an entire music curriculum. However, curriculum that omits any of these basic musical activities is incomplete, and incapable of producing the kind of comprehensive musician envisioned here.

SUGGESTED CURRICULUM

On the following pages a curriculum is suggested for students who have had Kodály training. It is assumed that the students for whom this curriculum is intended possess basic music reading and writing skills, can manage somewhat proficiently in solfa, and can sing in tune. Since these assumptions can rarely, in fact, be made with total accuracy, the first task must be to make them a reality.

Getting Started: How to create a functioning class from students with diverse and, possibly, limited musical backgrounds. Sometimes I think I spend my entire life just *beginning again.* Many years ago I came back from my second trip to Hungary, full of enthusiasm to incorporate the wonderful teaching techniques I had been observing into my new school program in Baltimore County, Maryland. In my mind's eye I saw myself doing *ti-ta*'s and *so-mi*'s with grade one, singing two-part Kodály choruses with grade four and performing Renaissance madrigals with grade six.

I will never forget the consternation with which I watched my sixth grade file into the music room that first week in September—their hands full of rock records. It appeared that the teacher before me had allowed them simply to sit around and listen to whatever music they chose to bring in during music period, as long as they didn't make any problems for him. He bribed their good behavior by letting them decide on curriculum. I realized that before I could do anything else I had to do battle with some very basic misconceptions held by these large and somewhat intimidating children.

The first idea I had to get across was:

You are the students and I am the teacher. I will teach—that's my job. You will learn—that's your job.

The second idea was:

> *What is to be learned, that is, the curriculum, is my decision, not yours. And there is a curriculum—a body of subject matter, skills, and knowledge to be acquired; and concepts to be inferred.*

The third idea was:

> *I will not bribe you to give me good behavior. I will praise you when you deserve praise. I will let you know very quickly and clearly when I find your behavior unacceptable.*

The fourth idea was:

> *I am not providing entertainment. You must go to your TV or radio for that. I am providing music education.*

I did not put these thoughts into words for the students. But I did let them know these things very surely through my actions and my behaviors toward them.

That day when they first came, fists full of records, I looked down at my completely unrealistic plan and said, "Oh, dear! I'm afraid we may not get to your records. We have a great deal to do today." Then I proceeded to lead them through a number of activities that required skill and thought: beat tapping, rhythm clapping, beat/rhythm switch, ostinato clapping as accompaniment to song, canon singing, inner-hearing exercises.

They could do none of them well. I shook my head frequently and said things like "my, we have got a lot of work ahead of us" and "dear me, you should have had that in third grade." I interspersed such comments with a few good ones—particularly about the singing of those who were singing at the beginning. And I made clear that everyone was expected to sing. To the question, "Do we have to?" I answered "Of course, you have to. In math class you have to do math. In singing class you have to sing." To the one or two recalcitrants I said, "Would you rather sing with everyone else now or for me alone later?"

As you can imagine, I wasn't the most popular teacher in the school that September—at least, not with the older students. But there were very few hold-outs by mid-year. As the classes began to achieve, they began to enjoy; and behavior problems all but disappeared.

Many of our problems in working with older beginners arise because we take what they say at face value, rather than translating what they say into what they mean. For example: "I don't like singing" means "I'm afraid to sing. I feel insecure about my voice; I'm afraid my friends will laugh at me if I sing." The solution for this is to insist that they sing. Then praise their singing and deal immediately and severely with any student who starts to laugh while another is singing.

Another example would be: "I don't like your kind of music. Why can't we sing our music [pop; rock] in music class?" This means: "It would be so much easier if I could just go on doing what I know already. Why must I work in music class?"

People like what they know. Students are bombarded with pop and rock music all their waking hours. Because the idiom is so familiar, they like it. It is up to us as music teachers to make other kinds of music—folk music and art music—familiar to our students. The sixth grade that appeared in September with rock records was asking to hear a favorite Bach composition in March.

I invented a beginning Kodály program for those youngsters. Since then I have had to teach older students with no Kodály background many times. The "Older Beginners" program I devised for them has been altered and refined many times.

The principles and philosophy of the Kodály Concept are as appropriate to older students as to younger ones. The use of the musical mother tongue, the folk songs, as the basic teaching material and of small range songs as a starting point—these are as valid with older students as with younger ones. As the five-year-old has a limited range and uncertain pitch, so has the untrained thirteen- to fifteen-year old, particularly the thirteen- to fifteen-year old boy. Simple folk melodies suit the adolescent voice as well as they suit that of the young child.

Of course, students who have never sung must first be led to sing and to enjoy singing. This alone can take months. However this time is well spent, since no musical learning can take place until the student has a repertory of familiar songs, from which to draw musical learning. Even after the repertory of songs is large and well established, the importance of moving systematically, making certain that each melodic and rhythmic pattern is learned thoroughly in all its variations before proceeding to the next one, cannot be stressed too much.

Older students intellectualize more easily than young children—but intellectualization and internalization are two different things. If the older student can tell you the names of the notes in a song but cannot sing, read, write, and improvise using these notes, he or she has not internalized musical learning. What that student knows is superficial fact, and is not musical learning at all.

The subject is still music. What we have to teach does not change just because students are older. Because they are older and are capable of abstract reasoning, we can teach some aspects of the subject much more quickly. There are few ten- or twelve-year-olds who cannot keep an accurate beat, for example.

Building a Repertory of Songs

Since musical learning must come from music, the first task must be to build a repertory of twenty to thirty folk songs, to the point where students can sing them well, accurately, and musically. This rote-taught repertory may be drawn from both pentatonic and diatonic music and should include examples in all common simple meters.[3] Students should have the music and text for these in their hands as they learn them. Older beginners come from a variety of backgrounds, but most will have seen notation at some point in their lives, and for a few, the notation may even be an aid to learning.

---

[3] Compound meters should be introduced as soon as a firm grounding in simple meters has been established.

This process is in sharp contrast to the Kodály Method for introducing notation to six or seven year olds—where nothing that has not been carefully prepared and brought to children's conscious knowledge may appear on the printed page. The twelve- or fifteen-year-old, however, has not been living in a vacuum for all of his or her school years. He or she will have seen notation in school series books, in church hymnals, and in countless other settings. Some students will have taken or be taking instrumental lessons. To refuse such a class access to printed notation is both pointless and self limiting.

In László Dobszay's excellent treatise on current practice in Hungary, *After Kodály*, he suggests:

> *[The teacher] demonstrates, sings for the class, leads the common performance of music and, parallel with this, always displays what is being done in written form. If they deal with music notation using the 'deciphering' method as well, the pupil will be able to identify more and more acoustic and visual components with gradually increasing precision. This may happen without threatening to destroy the inherent logic of music through stumbling across the difficulties of music reading....*[4]

If literacy can be taken to mean more than simply translating notes on a page into pitches, numerous activities that contribute to musical literacy can be undertaken while teaching this basic core of songs. As the students sing they may

learn about beat and meter.

- tap the beat.
- show accented beats.
- determine whether the music is moving in 2s, 3s or 4s.
- conduct the appropriate meter.

learn about tempo.

- sing the song in faster and slower tempi.
- determine what tempo is most suitable.
- learn correct tempo terminology: lento; adagio; moderato; vivace; presto....
- write the chosen tempo indication on their music.

---

[4] László Dobszay: *After Kodály, Reflection on Music Education*, pub. Zoltan Kodály Pedagogical Institute of Music, Kecskemét, 1992. pp.75-76.

learn about dynamics.

- sing the song louder and softer.
- decide on the most appropriate overall dynamic level.
- study the relationship of text to melodic rise and fall and determine if certain places in the music should be louder or softer.
- place traditional dynamic markings in their music based on their decisions:

learn about rhythm.

- clap the *way the words go*, the *rhythm*, while singing.
- identify that there are longer and shorter sounds and silences over the beat
- clap the rhythm while inner hearing the melody.
- clap the rhythm while singing, and on a signal from the teacher, switch to tapping the beat.

learn about pitch movement.

- show with hand levels (not hand-signs) the pitch movement, higher, lower, or repeated.
- diagram the melodic contours of the songs on paper or on the chalkboard.

learn about form.

- identify phrases in the song.
- tell which phrases are the same, which are different, and which are similar.
- with similar phrases tell what about them is the same and what is different.
- place A's, B's, and C's beside the song phrases to show the form of the song.

If these activities are pursued with most songs in the repertory, many basic literacy skills will have been acquired even though no conscious music reading may have taken place.

Introducing Rhythmic Notation

At this point, perhaps six weeks into the school year, it is possible to begin to focus on printed notation. The easiest starting point, as with younger students, is rhythm. It is both possible and desirable with older students to introduce three notational elements ♩, ♫, and 𝅗𝅥 in one lesson. Indeed, with older students, the comparison among these values appears to aid in learning them. Any duple or quadruple meter song containing only these rhythms will suffice. "Rocky Mountain" is a good example:

Focus first on the part that has "one sound on the beat":

Introduce the symbol ♩ and the syllable *ta* for one sound on one beat.

Then return to the beginning of the song and, tapping beats first, then clapping the rhythm, determine that there are "two sounds on each beat":

Introduce the symbol ♫, and the syllable *ti ti* for two sounds on a beat.

Next tap the beat while singing with words to determine "How many beats go by as we sing 'high'?' 'cry'?" (Two.)

Introduce the symbol $\downarrow$ and the syllable *too* for a sound that lasts for two beats. At this point the students should sing the entire song in *ta*'s, *ti*'s and *too*'s following the notation. Learning can be reinforced by singing other known songs containing these rhythmic elements, following the notation, and using the correct rhythm syllables. To reinforce the learning, the rhythm of a known song may be placed on the board in stem notation for the class to read in *ta*'s, and *ti*'s and then identify the song.

It is important to move quickly through all the common patterns of quarter notes, eighth note pairs, and half notes in duple and quadruple, and then in triple meter. While it is usual with younger children to move slowly pattern by pattern through the basic rhythms, this is neither necessary nor desirable with older students. The concept to be inferred is not *ti-ti*. The concept is that there may be one sound on a beat (the quarter note, which we sing as *ta*) two sounds on a beat (eighth notes, which we sing with *ti*) or one sound that last through two beats (the half note, which we sing with *too*). This concept may be generalized to all patterns of quarter notes, eight note pairs and half notes in simple duple, triple, and quadruple meters. Some patterns may require a bit more practice than others, but the understanding underlying them is the same.

Introducing *Solfa*

Solfa syllables may be introduced when basic rhythms are in place. Using a short, easy, five- note song the students know well, all five notes may be introduced in one lesson. Students should have copies of the music with the *solfa* indicated under the staff and a picture of the hand-signs on the same page.

ROCKY MOUNTAIN

FIGURE 1

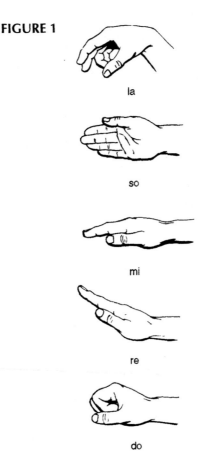

la

so

mi

re

do

The teacher sings the melody for the class in *solfa* and shows the hand-signs, with the class trying after. When the class seems generally secure, they should be instructed to memorize it: *Know it by next Tuesday. I will hear you sing it individually (or in duets or trios)*. Memorization as a skill has fallen into disrepute as an educational tool. In music, this is not only undeserved but also counterproductive. Memory is an essential skill in music, and like all skills, it must be practiced if it is to function well.

Once such an assignment is given it must be followed up. Students should be given opportunity to show what they have accomplished, and they should be praised when they perform well. Those who need more time should be given it. Smiling support and encouragement makes more willing learners than criticism. One technique that may help the slower students is to have students work together in teams. When a student is performing alone, his or her "team" must follow with inner hearing and be ready to jump in at a moments notice, singing the correct *solfa*. This spreading of the responsibility makes a game of what might otherwise be a stressful situation.

For the next few months, all songs are given with *solfa* written under the staff, and all are sung with *solfa* as an additional verse, either before or after the singing of the text.

This is wholly in keeping with Kodály's philosophy, as expressed in his preface to *Let Us Sing Correctly*:

Solmization should even precede acquaintance with musical notation.

This rote singing, over time, helps students aurally to associate *solfa* syllables with intervals and melodic turns. It is not music reading, but it is a step toward musical literacy. As the *solfa* becomes secure, it may be gradually withdrawn from the printed page. First it is omitted from the second of two phrases that are the same. Later it is written in under only the different parts of similar phrases, or in places where the interval or melodic turn is uncommon. Eventually it is not needed at all. However the teacher should not be surprised if students jot *solfa* into their music where it is missing. This is actually an encouraging sign. It is an indication that through the *solfa* they can decode the melody.

Beginning Melodic Reading and Writing

The Jaques-Dalcroze technique of a single-line, two-line or three-line staff is a useful one for beginning musical reading and writing with older students, and the Kodály volume, *333 Elementary Exercises*, is excellent beginning reading and writing material for older students. An easy example, (#1), is placed on the chalkboard in stem and *solfa* notation:

Music games are played until the exercise has been painlessly memorized:

1. All sing from the board notation in solfa and with hand signs.
2. Girls sing all the *do*'s, boys the *re*'s.
3. All sing, inner hearing (singing silently) all the *re*'s; then all the *do*'s.
4. All sing, clapping in canon at one-measure distance.
5. All sing, inner-hearing every other bar.

When the rhythm and melody are secure, the students may be given a page with just one line on it. They are told that that line is *do* and are instructed to notate what they have sung:

In another lesson, two lines are given and the students are asked to notate with do in the space:

d

From this the next step is the three-line staff and a *mi-re-do* exercise (#48):

As in the previous instance, musical games should be played until the exercise has been securely committed to memory. Then it may be notated by the students, first with *do* on a line and then with *do* in a space. From this the step to the five-line staff is a small one.

The process of writing tunes they know and then reading from their own notation should be a small part of every lesson. It is also a useful technique to leave bits of notation out of songs notated by the teacher for the class: *Oh dear! I seem to have left out the notes in the second phrase. What is the form? A A B A? Can you fill in the second phrase, please?* (There is a limit to the number of times this is believable. My students scan music immediately when they receive it to see what I've left out. They seem disappointed if it's all there.)

From three notes, extend music writing and reading to six-note stepwise movement of songs such as "Frère Jacques". Initially, keep reading and writing in keys that do not require key signatures: F, G, and C *do* for pentatonic songs and C *do* for songs with *fa* or *ti*.

Composing in the Classroom

Composition is a good activity for synthesizing learning. This may be begun early in the year and worked on for brief periods of time in many lessons throughout the year. Directions to the student might be:

1. Compose and notate a four-measure rhythm in 2/4. You may use quarter, eighth, and/or half notes. Use stem notation. Read your phrase to the class.
2. Get together with someone else. Combine your two rhythms into an A A B A form. Notate your composition by phrase in stem notation on the forms provided. Each of you should have a copy. (Figure 2)
3. Use dynamics to create a more interesting composition. You may use any of *p* or *f* or *crescendo* or *diminuendo*.
4. Decide on the tempo at which you want your composition performed. Use the correct musical tempo terminology.
5. Orchestrate your composition. You may use rhythm instruments or any other percussive sound source.
6. Practice your composition. Perform it for the class.

FIGURE 2
COMPOSITION BY

At this point it is easy to see the reason for having students work in pairs. Not only does partnering in the activity give the students more security, it also means fourteen performances to schedule rather than twenty-eight. If one allots only three minutes to a performance (adequate), this phase still occupies six minutes of every lesson for three weeks. The value in learning is more than worth the time, but time expenditures must be controlled. No more than five or six minutes of any period should be spent in compositional activities at any of the stages listed. It is easy to spend the whole period in such activities, but balanced musical learning is probably not best served in this way. In any case, work on compositions does not cease just because the music teacher has left. Students work on their projects at home, at lunch hour, at breaks, in the halls and on the school grounds. Composing is an engrossing activity.

Once melodic notation has been introduced, the rhythm compositions may be returned to and melodies added:

7. Add a melody to your rhythm. Put the *solfa* under the stem notation. You may use the notes *la-so-mi-re-do* for the A section and the notes *so-mi* for the B section. Make your composition end on *do*. (Or, if the teacher has introduced the concept of question-and-answer phrases: make your first A phrase a musical question and end it on *re* or *so*, make your second and fourth phrases answers and end on *do*.) As you compose, check to make sure that you can sing what you write.
8. Re-examine your tempo and dynamic markings. Do they fit well with the melody you have created? Make changes if you wish to.
9. Transfer your melody to the staff on the bottom of the page. Place it in F *do*.
10. Perform your composition for the class. You may sing it or play it on any melody instrument.

As the students progress, harmony parts, introductions, and codas may be added.

11. Add a second part to your composition. You may use any of: ostinato, descant, I and V chords or broken chords, or canon. Notate the second part.
12. Orchestrate your composition. You may use any of: the piano, xylophones and metalaphones, resonator bells, percussion instruments, or any other instrument you may have.
13. Practice your composition.
14. Perform for the class. Critique your own performance. Discuss your performance with the class. Hand in a fair copy of your finished composition to be placed in a notebook of class compositions.

Through composing, students take ownership of musical skills and knowledge. It should be stressed that the fourteen activities listed above may well take an entire year to accomplish.

Developing Readiness for Musical Theory

While the repertory of songs is being taught and concurrent with the teaching of beginning reading and writing skills, elementary music theory should be introduced. From the first singing of folk songs in *solfa*, tone sets for those songs should be placed on the chalkboard. For example, with "Rocky Mountain": "What is one note in this song?" "Another?" and "Another?" until all the pitches are on the board in whatever order they have been named. If an incorrect syllable is suggested, the class sings the song through in *solfa* to determine whether the suggested note is there. When all syllables have been named, the teacher asks a student to place them in order from lowest to highest, as a tone ladder:

la
so

mi
re
do

The teacher must take care that the spacing between *mi* and *so* reflects the minor third interval. The scale is then sung as steps and step-and-a-half:

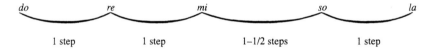

do	*re*	*mi*	*so*	*la*
1 step	1 step	1–1/2 steps	1 step	

Later, when *fa* and *ti* have been taught, the diatonic major scale pattern is constructed and sung to disclose its tetrachordal organization:

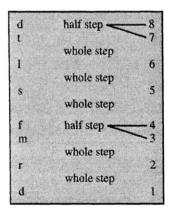

Still later, whole steps become major seconds and half steps become minor seconds in students' vocabularies. It helps to remind students that the archaic meaning of "major" is *big* and the meaning of "minor" is *little*. Major seconds are *big* seconds and minor seconds are *little* seconds. The tetrachord pattern when compared with absolute notes (the ABC's) makes the rationale for key signature clear:[5]

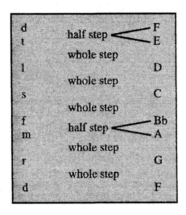

Major and minor seconds and thirds should be taught and practiced. A thirds drill may be used as a vocal warm-up.

With a solfa knowledge of the major scale, some rudimentary harmony may be introduced. This may take the form of singing the tonal center, *do*, as an ostinato with songs such as "Frére Jacques", with which it sounds harmonious, and labeling it I: tonic. Later songs with an implied V (such as "I's the B'y") should be sung and the need for another harmonic tone, *so*, discovered, labeled V: Dominant.

---

[5] An extensive discussion of the teachings of key signature may be found in *the Kodály Method, I: Comprehensive Music Education*, 3rd ed. (L. Choksy, Prentice Hall, 1998).

I'S THE B'Y

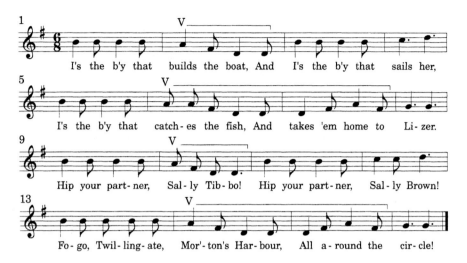

These harmonic tones, roots of the I and V chords, may be sung or played as a second part to many folk songs.

This small beginning of harmony and theory provide sufficient background for later teaching as the musical material of the lessons demand it.

Identifying and Classifying Music Sounds and Their Sources

One further aspect must be introduced to prepare older students for a more advanced music curriculum. While most students are familiar with some instrumental sounds, few come to the upper grades with a knowledge of how instrumental sounds are produced, or why certain instruments are grouped together in families.

From the beginning of the school year it is necessary to introduce instruments of the orchestra, one at a time, returning regularly to the basic concepts that:

1. the material of which a sound source is made affects the quality of the sound (timbre).
2. the playing mode (blowing, striking, bowing) affects the quality of the sound.
3. the means through which the sound is amplified affects its resonance (the bell on brass and woodwinds; the box under the strings; the chamber under the drums).
4. The size of the sound source affects its range, volume and pitch. (Larger = lower; smaller = higher)

By referring to the first three of these principles, instruments may be grouped into families. By referring to the fourth principle, instruments may be listed from highest to lowest voice within families. To view this information another way, instruments may be classified visually by material and size, aurally by timbre, and both aurally and visually by playing mode.

Instruments should be systematically introduced, through live performance wherever possible. Beginning band and orchestra students often make the best demonstrators. They more than make up in enthusiasm anything they may lack in skill. They can usually make their way through something the class is singing, and they happily explain how their instruments work, in terms easily understood by their contemporaries.

With the introduction of each new instrument the teacher should guide the students to consider the new instrument in terms of the four basic principles: material, playing mode, amplification method, and size. The instruments should be listed in student notebooks under the correct family heading as they are introduced:

Strings	*Brass*	*Woodwinds*	*Percussion*
Violin	Trumpet	Flute	Timpani
Viola	F. Horn	Oboe	Cymbals
Cello	Trombone	Clarinet	Xylophone
Double Bass	Tuba	Bassoon	Chimes

Of course it is not likely that all instruments can be introduced individually through live performance. For some, tapes or compact discs of performance accompanied by pictures, or videotapes may be substituted.

Compositions in which a theme is clearly played by first one orchestral family and then another, such as Benjamin Britten's *The Young Persons Guide to the Orchestra*, may prove helpful. Later, sections of works in which a theme is played by successive instruments in the same family will be useful. In the orchestral statement of the chorale theme in the last movement of Beethoven's Ninth *Symphony*, the theme—one easily singable by students—is played first by the double basses, next by the cellos and violas, and then by the violins. This movement through the string section from lowest to highest voiced instruments is extremely easy to follow. After it, the woodwinds, brasses and percussion join in, providing a clear sound map through the orchestra for students.

Aaron Copland's treatment of the Shaker tune "Simple Gifts" in his ballet suite *Appalachian Spring* is much the same, except that he begins with woodwinds—the simple solo sound of a clarinet, interspersed at one point with the oboe, and gradually moves to full orchestra.

In general, records, discs, and tapes purporting to do the job of teaching instruments of the orchestra for the teacher should be avoided. They tend to be cute and to use music of questionable quality.[6]

---

[6] An exception to this I have found in recent years is *The Orchestra*, by Mark Rubin and Alan Daniel (A Groundwood Book, pub. Douglas & McIntyre, Toronto, Vancouver, accompanied by audio tape. ISBN 0-88899-051-0) and the accompanying recording featuring Peter Ustinov and the Toronto Symphony. I recommend this for the upper elementary grades.

A Basic Teaching Guide for Introducing Orchestral Instruments

Pitch

1. Sound is the result of small movements called vibrations that set up sound waves of different frequencies (cycles). Three mediums which produce or enhance sound waves best are: the vibration of taut strings; the vibration of bells; and columns of air in tubes. One complete vibration is called a cycle. We can hear from 16 cycles to 20,000 cycles per second [the A above middle C is 440 cycles/second).

Teaching Method:

> Bass viol—watch the string vibrate.
> Resonator bells, xylophone—feel the bell vibrate.
> Stop the vibration by touching the bell or bar or string and hear the pitch stop.

2. Sounds can be higher or lower, or can repeat. This is called pitch. Size of the vibrating area affects pitch. A smaller space in which to vibrate produces higher sounds; a larger space produces lower sounds.

Teaching Method:

> Students suggest examples from nature and environment of high pitches (birds, mice) and low pitches (thunder, motorcycle).
> Compare sizes of sound sources and discuss the relationship of size to pitch.
> Observe with instruments demonstrated that:
>> Width: fatter strings or pipes produce lower pitches; thinner strings or pipes produce higher pitches.
>> Length: shorter = higher; longer = lower.
>> Strings: pluck a taut string. Pinch it in half and pluck it again (octave above produced).
>> Wind: Bottles of water. Blow across tops.

Tone Color

1. The quality of a sound (timbre, tone color) is affected by the material of which the sound source is made (wood, brass, skin, etc.) and the way the sound is produced (bowed, plucked, blown, hit, and so forth) Timbre depends on the amount and proportions of overtones present. The flute produces few overtones (pure sound). The violin produces many overtones (rich sound).

Teaching Method:

> Play and listen to and describe wood sounds (blocks, xylophone) and metal sounds (metallophone).

Identify as wood sounds or metal sounds when heard but not seen.
Fill bottles with water. Striking the bottle produces a bell sound; blowing
  across the mouth of the bottle produces a wind sound.
Pluck strings or bow strings.
Blow into a garden hose with a brass mouthpiece.

Dynamics

1. Loudness depends upon how hard the instrument is struck, plucked, blown into,
   and so on. (the amplitude of the vibration).

Teaching Method:

Experiment with plucking hard, lightly; blowing softly, forcefully.

2. A box added to some instruments gives the sound waves more place to vibrate,
   which can make the sound louder. The sound box provides a resonating air
   chamber to amplify the sound. Examples: violin, cello, bass, harp (alongside or
   at bottom), drums, etc.). A chamber under the striking surface makes the sound
   louder, amplifies it.

Summary

Pitch

1. Sound is the result of vibrations.
2. Sounds can be higher or lower (pitch)
3. Size of the vibrating area affects pitch. A smaller area produces a higher pitch.
   A larger area produces a lower pitch.

Timbre/Tone Color

1. Tone color is affected by the material of which the sound source is made.
2. Tone color is affected by the way the sound is produced (playing method).

Dynamics

1. Loudness depends upon how hard the instrument is plucked, blown into,
   struck, and so on.
2. A resonating air chamber amplifies sound. (A box underneath or beside the instrument can make it louder.)

Conclusion

The work described in this chapter can be accomplished in one school year if the students begin with a smattering of musical knowledge and simply need to be given focus, a common musical vocabulary, and some additional understanding.[7] If the students are truly beginners, and the music class meets only twice weekly, the material of this chapter may well require another half year of study.

This is a comprehensive course of study whether used as review or as new teaching material. It encompasses fully the fourfold curriculum base of performing, listening, analyzing and creating. It can provide the necessary background for any more advanced study in music. It is a readiness curriculum designed to open the world of music to students.

---

[7] The plan given in this chapter is essentially the one used by the author with sixth-grade students at St. Rita's School, Calgary, in 1993–94.

Chapter 2

Putting It All Together: 19 Sample Lessons for Getting Older Students Started

CONSTRUCTING LESSONS

One of the most difficult tasks facing teachers is the planning of day-to-day, class-to-class lessons. It is easy to be overwhelmed by the mass of material to be covered.

A "good" lesson must, like a good piece of music, contain elements of both unity and variety. It must have form and content and there should be a thread running through it that makes it flow without abrupt stops and starts. Variety in lessons can be achieved through both the music and the activities used to enhance the music. Unity comes from more subtle aspects—the use of the singing voice as the basis for all musical learning, solfa as an aid to reading and writing, and employment of consistent techniques of musical analysis. Unity may be achieved also through consistent shaping of lessons, always beginning with the familiar, moving to the new and challenging, and closing with the familiar.

The one-hour lessons given here were originally constructed for use with a mixed age group of eighteen musically talented students at Mount Royal Conservatory. These students were all instrumentalists in a scholarship program. Most could read music instrumentally but not vocally and most had done little singing or music writing previously. None had previously used solfa.

During the period that these lessons were being used with this group of children they were also being tested in an only slightly different format with 32 sixth graders in a Calgary public school.[1] Each "lesson" taught in one hour at Mount Royal took two 45 minutes periods with this unselected class of sixth graders. Lessons were essentially divided in half and given new opening and closing sections.

The lessons worked equally well with the selected class at the Conservatory and the unselected class in the schools. They are offered here as one way of organizing teaching on a lesson-by-lesson basis so that through the activities of singing, mov-

---

[1] St. Rita's School in Northwest Calgary is in the Catholic School System. In Calgary the Catholic Schools are supported with tax funding and are thus "public."

ing, playing instruments, reading, writing, listening, and creating, students of any age or background may be led to infer concepts and develop skills in all the elements of music.

TEACHING TOWARD CONCEPT INFERENCE AND SKILL DEVELOPMENT

There is considerable confusion in the literature as to what a "concept" is and how concepts may be "taught." A concept is a major idea, understanding, or generalization that can be applied to many diverse situations. "Over-the-beat music moves in longer and shorter sounds and silences" is a rhythmic concept that is as true of Stravinsky's *Rite of Spring* as it is of "Bye Baby Bunting." It is an important understanding for students to hold. Concepts cannot however be "taught." Skills may be taught. We can teach students to sing, play, move, listen, and create. But we cannot teach students to "understand".

The teacher can only present carefully selected experiences through which the students may understand, that is, infer correct concepts about music. For the teacher to do this requires that he or she clearly know what the fundamental musical concepts are. Only then can musical experiences be ordered sequentially so that students may be led to musical understanding. To this end, a list of fundamental musical concepts/understandings is given below.

Concepts to Be Inferred

MELODY is the result of a linear arrangement of pitches.

> Consecutive higher, lower, and repeated pitches may be organized into melodies.
> Pitch movement can be by step, skip, or leap to give melodies shape or contour.
> Pitches may be organized into patterns or motives.

RHYTHM is the movement of music.

BEAT
> Most music has a recurring underlying pulse called the beat.
> Beats can be subdivided into smaller groups of two's or three's.

METER
> Some beats have a feeling of stress or accent.
> Beats are organized into groups defined by accented beats.
> Beat groupings move in two's, three's, or combinations of two's or three's.

RHYTHM
> Over the beat music moves in longer and shorter sounds and silences.

Sounds and silences can be arranged evenly over beats.
Sounds and silences can be arranged unevenly over beats.
Rhythms may be organized into patterns or motives.

FORM is the organization or architecture of music.

Pitches and rhythms may be organized into small patterns or motives.
Music has built in resting places (phrase endings).
Phrases can be the same, different, or similar. Similar phrases have something that is the same and something that is different.
Phrases can sound finished or unfinished.
Phrases that sound unfinished are usually followed by phrases that sound finished (questions & answer).
Same, different, and similar phrases can be organized into patterns.
Same, different, and similar phrases can comprise the form of a whole piece or can become a section of more complex formal structures.
The qualities of same, different, and similar are used in music to achieve unity and variety, tension and release.
Larger compositions may include sections that serve to introduce or close the piece.
Larger compositions may include bridges that help form smooth transitions between sections.

TEMPO is the speed of the beat.

Beats in music can move either faster or slower.
Tempo can change either suddenly or gradually in music.
The character of the music is often underlined by the tempo.

DYNAMIC LEVEL is the volume at which music is performed.

Music can be louder or softer.
Dynamics can change suddenly or gradually.
As pitches ascend, there is a natural tendency to get louder, and as pitches descend, there is a natural tendency to get softer.
The character of the music is frequently underlined by the dynamics.

TIMBRE is the distinctive tone quality of each type of instrument or voice that sets it apart from others.

The larger the instrument is, the lower it will sound; the smaller the instrument, the higher the sound.
The quality of sound (i.e. tone color) is determined by:
The size of the sound's source.
The material of which the sound source is made.
The method by which the sound is produced (striking, blowing, plucking, etc.).

The resonating area.

The method of amplification.

HARMONY occurs when two or more pitches are produced simultaneously.

Two or more sounds may occur at the same time.

Music can be organized horizontally or vertically or in a combination of the two to produce harmony.

Simultaneous sounds can be organized to create a feeling of tension or release.

Sometimes a melody has a less important accompaniment that adds interest to the music (homophony).

Sometimes a melody can be combined with itself or other melodies to produce harmonies (polyphony).

Concepts are the understandings we hold about each of the elements of music: melody, rhythm, harmony, form, tempo, timbre, and dynamics. Skills are our abilities for performance. Both concept inferences and skills are developed through musical experiences: singing, playing instruments, moving, reading, writing, and creating.

For this reason, lessons should present a balance between skill formation and concept inference activities. The following lessons are constructed in such a way that skills may be developed and enhanced and musical understanding increased.

MOUNT ROYAL CONSERVATORY—LESSON 1

A. Basic Rhythmic Vocabulary

1. "Rocky Mountain"

- teach by rote
- tap beats
- clap rhythm
- introduce rhythm syllables
- review: one sound on a beat
  two sounds on a beat
  one sound lasts two beats
- sing with *ta*, *ti*, and *too*

Rhythm repeat: teacher taps rhythm by phrase; students clap, then say each phrase.

Read rhythms from flash cards

B. Solfa and Hand-Signs

2. "Brother John"

- review with text; sing in canon
  * Vocabulary term: canon
- introduce solfa syllables and hand-signs—"Let's make a scale"—place solfa discs on board in random order and have students come to board to arrange the discs from low to high. Practice scale ascending and descending. Ending note? (*do*)
- sing with solfa and handsigns

C. Meter

3. "Yankee Doodle"

- Rote teach. How many beats in the first phrase? (8) Diagram on board.

Bounce balls to find accents.
- How is it moving? Mark accents under the hearts.
- Place bar lines.
- Draw concept inference: accent determines meter.
- Conduct 2s while singing.

4. "I've Been to Haarlem"

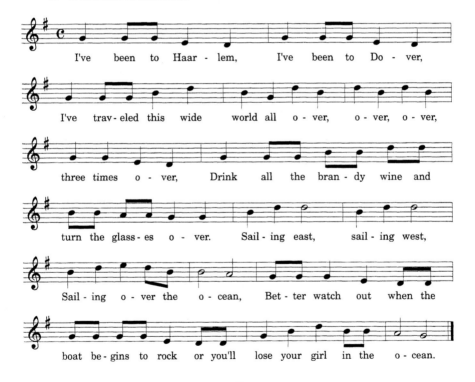

- teach by rote; perform dance[2]
- how is it moving? (4s)
- teach conducting gesture for (4s)

---

[2] Lois Choksy and David Brummitt, *120 Singing Games and Dances*, (Englewood Cliffs, N.J.: Prentice Hall, 1987).

D. Tonal Center

5. "Eyes of Blue"

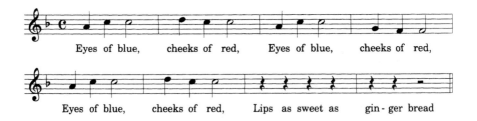

- Teach by rote. Teach melody and text for the first three phrases. For the fourth phrase, speak the text in rhythm without melody. Have students improvise a melody for the last phrase. The only rule is that it must end on *do*.

E. Game

6. Categories: Instruments

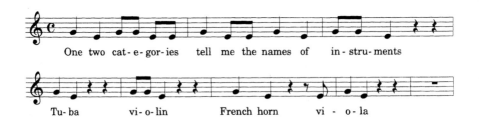

Directions: The class sings the first part of this song. Individual students supply the names of the instruments. If someone is unable to come up with another instrument name, the category is changed, e.g., to composers.

HOMEWORK:

1. Be able to sing: "Rocky Mountain" and "Brother John" with *solfa* and hand-signs.
2. Compose an ending to "Eyes of Blue". Notate it or just think of an ending and be prepared to sing it.

* Strike the tuning fork against the board so that the class can hear and sing the "A" sound. Sing the A as re; find *do* (G) This should be done by the teacher with the students.

A. Meter

1. "Rocky Mountain"

- sing and conduct 2s
- sing with rhythm syllables—individual performances
  change tempo from moderato to adagio to vivace
  *Vocabulary terms: tempo, moderato, adagio, vivace
- sing in *solfa* with hand-signs—place the tone ladder on the board—ending note? (*do*)

2. What do bar lines tell us? (How the music is moving.)

- New Song: "Lavender's Blue"

La - ven - der's   blue,   dil - ly,   dil - ly,   La - ven - der's   green,

When you   are   King,   dil - ly,   dil - ly,   I shall be   queen.

*Vocabulary term: accent

- "Find the meter. How is the music moving?"

- draw accent marks - then bar lines for $\frac{3}{4}$
- conduct in 3s while singing

B. Dynamics

3. "Brother John"

- sing in unison and in canon
- sing with *solfa*/handsigns - individual performance - tone ladder on board; ending note? (*do*)

- sing with text, conduct 4s
- change "dynamics" - from mf to ff to pp
  *Vocabulary term: dynamics

C. Form

4. Rhythm Erase ("Rain, Come Wet Me")

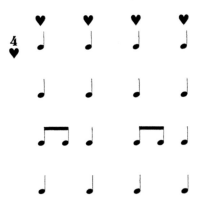

a. Are any phrases the same? Label these "A." Any different? Label "B."
The form of this piece is AABA.

* Vocabulary term: form

b. memorize/say
c. reconstruct on the board
d. "Rain, Come Wet Me"

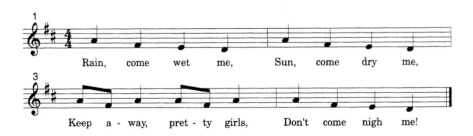

- teach by rote
e. derive *solfa* - ending note? (*do*)
f. place *solfa* notation under each phrase on the board
g. have students sing in *solfa* with hand-signs

D. Compose

5. "Eyes of Blue"

- class sings first three phrases; individual students sing the endings they improvised or composed.

6. "I've Been to Haarlem"

- teacher claps the rhythm ♩♫♩♩ | ♩♩♫♩♩
- what song goes this way?
- students sing from notation using rhythm syllables
- what is the ending note? (*do*)

7. Categories - instruments; composers

HOMEWORK: Continue to work on "Rocky Mountain" in *solfa*

MOUNT ROYAL CONSERVATORY—LESSON 3

Tuning Fork A = *mi*; find *do* (F)

A. Review Meter

1. "Lavender's Blue"

Sing with:
- text; conduct 3s
- rhythm syllables
- *solfa* and hand-signs
- what is last note? (*do*) this is called the tonal center.

* Vocabulary term: tonal center

2. "Brother John"

Sing with:
- text and conduct 4s
- *solfa* and handsigns

3. What do bar lines tell us? (accent)

- where is the bar line - accent in "**Brother John**"?
- suppose we were to change "**Brother John**" to $\frac{2}{4}$ or $\frac{3}{4}$?
- conduct and sing in $\frac{2}{4}$; in $\frac{3}{4}$

B. Review *Solfa*

4. "Rain Come Wet Me"

- identify by hand-signs shown by the teacher
- sing with text
- sing in *solfa*
- sing with rhythm syllables
- notate rhythm

5. Kodály 333, Exercise 48

- read rhythm from board
- read *solfa* from board
- memorize
- inner hear all the *re*'s
- inner hear all the *do*'s
- boys sing the *do*'s; girls the *re*'s

C. Pentatonic Scales

6. "Rocky Mountain"

- derive scale and label as "*do* pentatonic"

* Vocabulary terms: scale, pentatonic

7. Laughing Canon (See Page 111)

- teach by rote process; text and *solfa*
- preparation for diatonic major Scale

8. Categories - instruments; composers

HOMEWORK: Memorize "Laughing Canon" with *solfa* and hand-signs.

Fork A = *so*; find *do* (D)

A. Review Meter, Rhythm, Solfa

1. "Lavender's Blue"

- sing text, show accented/unaccented beats—"How is the music moving?"
- conduct 3s
- sing with *solfa* and handsigns
- construct scale with discs on board
  - what is the last note? (*do*)
  - what is the tonal center? (*do*)
  - how many notes are in this scale? (6)

2. "Rocky Mountain"

- sing text, show accented/unaccented beats—"How is the music moving?"
- conduct 2s
- sing with *solfa* and hand-signs
- sing and inner hear all *mi*'s
- construct and label scale on board, using *solfa* discs
  - what is the last note? (*do*)
  - what is the tonal center? (*do*)
  - how many notes are in this scale? (5)
  - what is it called? (*do* pentatonic)

3. "Land of the Silver Birch"

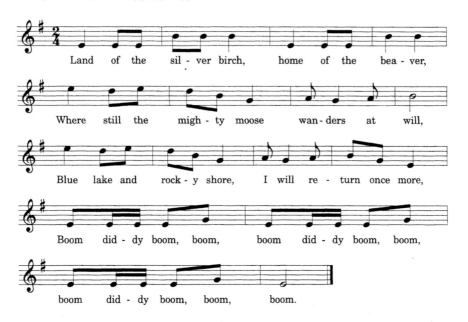

- new song, teach by rote, discuss text, show phrases by moving right arm left to right for each (teacher use left arm to present correct mirror image)
- show the accented/unaccented beats—"How is the music moving?" (4s)
- conduct in 4s

4. "Ghost of John"

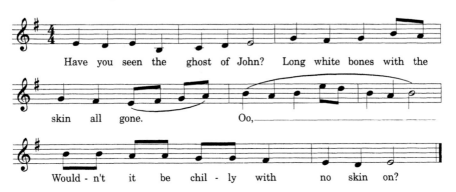

- new song, teach by rote
- use third phrase as an ostinato
  * Vocabulary term: ostinato

- have individuals sing third phrase
- sing in canon   a)   class sings, teacher enters in canon
                         b)   teacher sings, class enters in canon
                         c)   1/2 class sings, 1/2 class enters in canon
                         d)   reverse parts

5. Kodály 333

- review; sing with rhythm syllables with solfa and hand-signs, notate on one-line staff on paper

6. Laughing Canon

- sing with text
- all sing in *solfa* with hand-signs
- sing in canon using the "canon process" (see above under "Ghost of John")
- teacher adds third voice if the students are secure in 2 parts

7. Categories - composers

HOMEWORK: Memorize "Ghost of John" with text and rhythm syllables.

MOUNT ROYAL CONSERVATORY—LESSON 5

1. **Think the sound of "A"**—now sing it. Check with tuning fork (teacher sounds tuning fork on board staff).

   - "Were we correct? Too high? Too low?" Call A "*re*"; find *do*. Begin "Rocky Mountain" on this *do*.

2. **"Rocky Mountain"**

   - sing with text and conduct 2s
   - sing with *solfa* and hand-signs
   - what is the last note? tonal center? (*do*)
   - what is the scale? (*do* pentatonic)
   - arrange discs on board for *do*-pentatonic scale
   - review: what is a scale? (an ordering of all the notes in song from lowest to highest)
     * Vocabulary term: scale

3. **"Lavender's Blue"**

   - sing with text and conduct 3s
   - sing with *solfa* and hand-signs
   - have student add *fa* to the pentatonic scale on the board to make the correct scale for this song
   - show *mi-fa* close together on the tone ladder
   - scale? *do-la* with *mi-fa* half step (semitone); this is a 6-note scale; it is no longer "pentatonic."

4. **"Laughing Canon"**

   - sing with text in unison
   - sing with solfa and hand-signs
   - what notes must we add to the scale for this song? (*ti* and *do*)
   - have a student construct on board with discs. Note t-d semitone/half step
   *• label major scale, *do-do*[1]
   - sing the song as a two-part canon

5. **"Land of the Silver Birch"**

   - review and sing for expression and phrasing
   - add ostinato on "boom-diddy" part
   - sing in 2 parts
   - derive the scale as *la* ending; *la* pentatonic

6. "Ghost of John"

- check homework
- sing with text—work on expressive singing
- sing with rhythm syllables
- try in canon
- ending note? (*la*)
  * Vocabulary term: minor
- have we sung any other songs today that sound like they might be minor? That is, end on *la*? ("Silver Birch") (Check answers by singing in solfa)
- construct natural minor scale beside major scale on the board and compare the two

7. "Old Brass Wagon"

- teach by rote
- perform dance[3]

HOMEWORK: be able to sing 2 scales "major" and "natural minor" with *solfa* and hand-signs.

---

[3] See *120 Singing Games and Dance*, Choksy and Brummitt, for directions.

MOUNT ROYAL CONSERVATORY—LESSON 6

On Board: Solfa Discs for two scales, major and natural minor

1. A = *so*; **find** *do* - what key are we in? (D = *do*)
2. **Sing major and natural minor scales** beginning on D with *solfa* and hand-signs

   - focus on "major seconds/minor seconds"
     * Vocabulary term: major seconds = big seconds; minor seconds = little seconds.

3. **Major/Minor: "Brother John"**

   - teacher sings first in major and then in minor
   - how was this song different the second time? (It was in minor.)
   - what makes the minor scale sound different? At which scale step do we know it is minor?
   - the teacher sings first the major scale and then the minor scale beginning on the same starting pitch.
   - the difference is at the third step. It is lower in minor.

4. **Kodály 333, 48**

   - sing from memory
   - notate on a three-line staff, first with *do* in a space, then with *do* on a line.

5. **Prepare for Listening** (sing in F = *do*)

   Board:

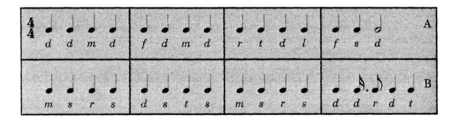

   a. the form is a a b a - read the rhythm in this form
   b. read in *solfa*
   c. memorize
   d. "What is it?" (They will not know.)

e. "I'll sing the other part—maybe that will help you recognize it" (teacher sings "Twinkle, Twinkle Little Star").

f. "You sing my part now and I'll sing yours."

g. Half class sing upper voice/half lower
   Information: this arrangement is by Mozart in a set of variations "Ah Vous Dirai-je Maman."

h. What does "vary" mean? "variation"? How could we vary this tune and still keep it recognizable?
   Rhythmically?
   - more sounds on the beat
   - less sounds on the beat
   - uneven arrangements of sounds

   Melodically?
   - notes in between
   - decorations
   - octave displacement

   Mode?
   - major to minor

   Accompaniment?
   - chords, broken chords

   Try each suggestion.

   * Vocabulary terms: vary and variation

HOMEWORK: Compose a rhythmic variation on "Twinkle, Twinkle Little Star."

6. **"Old Brass Wagon"**—sing and perform dance
7. **Categories**—composers

A = *mi*; **find** *do*;

(1) sing major and minor scales from D
(2) review "major seconds," "minor seconds"

A. Review Rhythmic Concepts

1. "Chairs to Mend"

- teach by rote. Sing in canon
- sing with hand-signs and *solfa*
- perform with ostinato ♩ ♫ ♩ ♩

2. Review Rhythmic Concepts

- sounds may be arranged:
  1) evenly (♩ ; ♫) over beats
  2) or may be longer (♩ ; ♩ ♩) than beats; we can tie notes of shorter

  duration together to make longer sounds

B. Compose

- sing "Twinkle, Twinkle Little Star"
- discuss "rhythmic variation"
- perform the rhythmic variations composed by the students

C. Notate

Kodály 333, 48
- sing from memory
- notate twice on five-line staff: *do* on second line; then *do* in first space

D. Review

    3. "Ghost of John"

         • sing in canon

    4. "Land of the Silver Birch"
    5. "Old Brass Wagon"

         • sing
         • perform dance
         • derive ♪♪♪♪ - four sounds on one beat; *tika tika*

    6. Categories - instruments/composers

G = *so*; find *do*

A. Rhythm: Uneven Arrangement of Sounds over Beats

1. "Chairs to Mend"

- sing with text/conduct 4s
- sing in canon
- sing and clap ostinato
- Questions: Is the ostinato the same as the singing rhythm? (No.)
  Where is it different? (Chairs.)
  How is it different? (Chairs is a longer sound.)
  How could we change the notation of our ostinato without erasing anything so that when we perform it, it will sound the same as our singing rhythm? (Tie the *ta* to the first *ti*.)

2. "Alabama Gal"

Ain't I   rock can - dy,   Ain't I   rock can - dy,

Ain't I   rock can - dy,   Al - a - bam - a - gal.

- rote teach
- perform with ostinato
- perform dance

B. Compose

3. Variations on "Twinkle, Twinkle Little Star"

- hear performances by the students of their rhythmic variations
- have class critique; the rule for criticism is: first, find something good to say and then suggest how something might be made better

C. Major and Minor Seconds

4. "Whistle, Daughter" (preparation for F-*do*, one flat and other key signatures)

WHISTLE, DAUGHTER

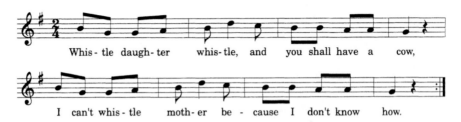

Whis- tle daugh- ter   whis- tle, and   you shall have a   cow,

I can't whis - tle   moth- er be - cause I don't know   how.

- create new verses

5. Intervals

- major and minor seconds and thirds. The old meaning of "major" is big and of minor is "little". Any two notes next door to each other in the scale are "seconds," e.g.
- look at the tone ladder:

- are all seconds the same size? (No. Some are big seconds [major] and some are little seconds [minor], e.g. *fa-mi* and *ti-do*.)
- sing the scale and name the seconds
  mi to *fa* is a minor second etc...
  re to *mi* is a major second.
  do to *re* is a major second.
- if we count up or down three notes, the interval is a third.

3 m	3 f
2 (r)	2 (m)
1 d	1 r

- are all thirds the same size? (No. Some are big thirds, major, and some are little thirds, minor).
- sing the consecutive thirds drill

d   m   r   f   m   s   f   l

s   t   l   d   t   r   d

d   l   t   s   l   f   s   m

f   r   m   d   r   t   d

6. **Categories** - composers

HOMEWORK: Memorize the thirds drill.

A = *so*; find *do*.

Sing thirds drill as a class and then around the room, each student in turn on the next third. Try to maintain a steady beat.

A. Rhythm: Uneven Arrangements of Sounds over Beats

1. "Chairs to Mend"

- sing text and conduct 4s
- sing in canon
- review  as

2. "Alabama Gal"

- review song; conduct in 2s
- play game
- sing and clap ostinato
- Questions: Is the ostinato the same as the song rhythm? (No.)
  Where is it different? ("I" in the verse "Ain't I Rock Candy.")
  How is it different? ("I" is a longer sound.)
  How could we change the notation of our ostinato without erasing anything so that when we perform it, it will sound the same as our singing rhythm? (Tie the second and third *ti*'s together:

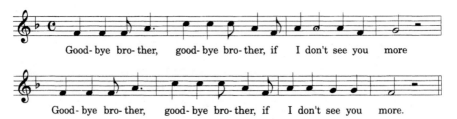

3. New Song: "Good-bye Brother"

Good-bye bro-ther,   good-bye bro-ther, if   I don't see you   more

Good-bye bro-ther,   good-bye bro-ther, if   I don't see you   more.

- rote teach; put students' names in text

- teacher claps ostinato ♪ ♩ ♪ ♩ ♩
- students identify as   ti ta   ti   ta ta
- place on board
- students clap/teacher sings
- students clap and sing
- derive ♪ ♩. pattern through the tie using the above (#2) questions

4. Review rhythmic concepts

- sounds may be evenly arranged over the beats
- sounds may be unevenly arranged over beats
- sounds may last longer than a single beat (full beats)

B. Listening

5. "Twinkle, Twinkle Little Star"

- class sing upper voice—student plays lower on piano
- review the kinds of rhythms used in the students' variations (uneven, longer, even)
- let's hear how Mozart used rhythmic variation
- listen to tell what rhythmic patterns you hear
- play and discuss the first two variations

6. Melodic Variations, "Twinkle, Twinkle Little Star"

- how could we vary this melody?
  - notes in between
  - decorations
  - major/minor
  - upside down
  - other?

HOMEWORK: create a melodic variation

A = *so*; **find** *do* **(D) Sing the Thirds Drill in unison and individually by memory**

A. Major/Minor Seconds and Thirds

1. "Whistle, Daughter"

- create verses
- derive rhythm and *solfa*/relate to tone ladder
- place on board
- find the thirds in the melody

B. Discuss Elements of Music

- duration (beat/rhythm/meter), pitch movement (melody/tune), tempo, dynamics, form, simultaneous sounds (harmony), timbre/tone color
- any musical element may be used to vary the music—to create a "variation"

C. Compose

3. "Twinkle, Twinkle"; Melodic Variation

- how did we create melodic variations?
- decorations, trills
- notes in between melody notes
- octave displacement
- major/minor
- perform students' melodic variations
- how else could we vary this music? (add other parts - harmony)

4. Read and Sing "Twinkle, Twinkle Little Star," Inner Voice

- sing without ties, repeating the notes
- sing with ties

5. "Twinkle, Twinkle Little Star"

- students sing upper and lower voices
- teacher sings the above inner voice while class sings upper and lower voices
- review "variation" rhythmic variation, melodic variation, harmonic variation
- listen to Mozart Variation #2. Can you find the part we have been singing?

6. "Rocky Mountain"

- sing with text
- sing in *solfa*

- identify triad on d-m-s; how constructed? (major 3rd, minor 3rd—1-3-5 on *do*)

* Vocabulary term: triad, chord

- sing d-m-s consecutively then together as a "chord"
- label: "the triad on *do*," "I," "tonic"

HOMEWORK: Memorize the inner voice for "Twinkle, Twinkle Little Star."

A = *so*: find *do* (Do)

Sing thirds drill

1. Aural/Oral Thirds Identification

- sing and memorize

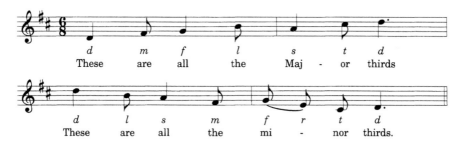

d	*m*	*f*	*l*	*s*	*t*	*d*	
These	are	all	the	Maj -	or	thirds	
d	*l*	*s*	*m*	*f*	*r*	*t*	*d*
These	are	all	the	mi -	nor	thirds.	

2. "Rocky Mountain"

- sing with text
- sing in *solfa*
- pull out words of phrase 3: *do, do, do (do-mi-so)*
- sing consecutively and then together as a chord
- label "I chord", "I triad", "tonic"
- note appearance on staff; always line-line-line, or space-space-space

3. "I's the B'y" (See Page 19)

- teach by rote
- sing in solfa
- is there a triad (line-line-line or space-space-space) any place in this song? (6 times)
- on what solfa note is this triad built? (*so*)
- what degree of the scale is *so*? (5)
- label the triad on *so* as V, Dominant
- sing the V triad pitches consecutively and as a three-part chord

4. Locate other triads by looking at the scale on the board

- label each with the number of its root
- are all triads the same? Look at the interval from 1 to 3. Sometimes this is a big third (major), other times a little third (minor).
- Rule: If the bottom third in a triad is major, the triad is major. We use a capital Roman numeral—I, IV, V, etc. If the bottom third in a triad is minor, the triad is minor. We use a lowercase Roman numeral—ii, vi, etc.

5. Sing the triads drill (See page 47)

- label each triad with the correct Roman numeral

6. "Ah Vous Dirai-je Maman"

- sing in three parts with inner voice
- listen to Variations III and IV; discuss how the tune is varied in these
- collect and perform remaining student melodic variations

7. "Whistle, Daughter, Whistle"

- sing student-created verses
- sing with rhythm syllables
- place rhythm notation on chalkboard

8. Categories Game - elements of music

HOMEWORK: Memorize the triads drill; be able to identify each triad as major or minor.

A = *so*; find *do* (D) Sing the Triads drill

A. Tetrachords and the Diatonic Major Scale

   1. "Chairs to Mend"

- sing text, conduct 4s
- derive *solfa*
- place the scale on the board

   2. "Whistle, Daughter"

- text - make up verses
- *solfa* - place the scale on the board

   3. New Song: "Haul on the Bow Line"

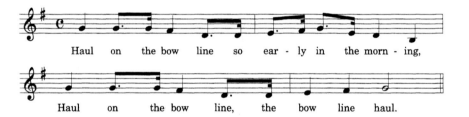

Haul on the bow line so ear - ly in the morn - ing,

Haul on the bow line, the bow line haul.

- teach by rote
- derive *solfa*
- place scale on board

   4. Compare above scales

- discover "matching" tetrachords"

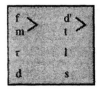

B. Triads and Chords

5. Review Tonic Triad (I)

- pull from first phrase of "Rocky Mountain"

6. Use Tonic Triad as an accompaniment for "Brother John"

- sing the triad or play it on piano or xylophone

7. Review "I's the B'y"

- use *do* (I) and *so* (V) as second voice-part with the song:
- mark I and V in the music to show where chord changes occur

A = *la*, find *do* (C). Sing diatonic major scale, ascending and descending, in *solfa* and absolutes.

1. New Song: Cherubini Canon No. 2

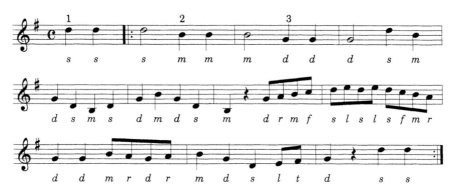

- listen as teacher sings
- read phrase-wise, teacher helps as needed.
- find I triads and chords in the melody.
- what is the difference between a "triad" and a "chord"?
  - A triad is always 1-3-5, but in a chord the notes of the triad may appear in another order. Triads always have three notes, chords may have more.

Hearing Implied Harmonies

2. "I's the B'y"

- review text
- *solfa* and hand-signs
- accompany with *do*; I and *so*, V
- review V triad in the melody. r-t-s
- review triad = line-line-line or space-space-space
- sing accompanying with I and V triads. Discover need for inversion to make good voice leading:

```
s ——————— s ——————— s
m ——————— r ——————— m
d ——————— t ——————— d

I ——————— V ——————— I
```

3. "Whistle, Daughter"

- sing with student-created verses
- refer to tetrachord d r m f
- relate to absolutes in C = *do*
- relate to absolutes in F = *do*
- discover the need for the flat in F = *do* to create the correct tetrachord pattern:

f	B♭
m	A
r	G
d	F

4. "Miss Mary Mack"

- sing and play game
- place scale on board in *solfa* and absolutes in C = *do*

d	C
t	B
l	A
s	G

- now move *do* to G:

d	G
t	F#
l	E
s	D

- discover the need for a sharp in the key of G to create the tetrachord pattern

5. Categories - large forms (concerto, symphony, sonata, etc.)

A = *so*; find *do* (D)

A. Review scales and key signatures

1. Construct scale on board and sign in *solfa*

- add absolutes for D = *do*
- discover need for another sharp:

d'	D
t	C#
l	B
s	A
f	G
m	F#
r	E
d	D

- sing absolutes for D = *do*

B. Review Major and Minor Triads

2. Cherubini Canon No. 2

- sing in canon
- pull out I chord
- review definitions of "triad" and "chord"; how different?

3. Triad Drill

- triads all the same? (refer to scale on board) - No.
- how different? - Some have a Major third on the bottom, others have a minor third on the bottom. The third between one and three determines the Majorness or minorness of the triad.
- label triads from I to vi as Major or minor

4. "I's the B'y"

- sing from memory
- *solfa* and handsigns
- what triad is outlined in the melody? (V)
- Major or minor? (Major)
- review Triad as line-line-line or space-space-space

C. Prepare for Listening

5. New: Beethoven Symphony No. 6, The *Pastorale*, 5th Movement (See page 122)

- read the theme
- memorize
- give brief historic background on Beethoven

HOMEWORK: Look up "Beethoven." Be ready to tell one thing about him at the next class.

A = *do*

A. Scales

1. Construct and sing an A major scale:

d'	A
f	G#
l	F#
s	E
f	D
m	C#
r	B
d	A

B. Triads and Chords

2. Cherubini Canon No. 2

- sing in canon
- pull out I triad
  - place on board in key of C - class sings
  - what will happen if we invert this triad?
    - 1st inversions (6) chord
    - 2nd inversion $\binom{6}{4}$ chord

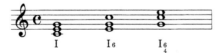

C. Prepare for Listening: Analyze Harmony

3. Beethoven Symphony No. 6, The *Pastorale*, Finale

- harmonize with *do* and *so*

- does this harmonization seem to fit? (not in all places)
- listen to Beethoven bass line (they sing upper voice, teacher sings the bass line). (See page 126)

    Students sing the bass line while teacher sings melody.

    Conclusion: Beethoven used some other chords
- Students report on their readings

D. Discover the IV chord

4. New Song: "Lumberman's Alphabet" (See page 100)

- sing with text
- sing in *solfa*
- discover the "triad" in the melody
- what number? (IV) f-l-d

5. Sing chord progressions using the IV chord:

$$\text{I} \quad \text{IV}_6^4 \quad \text{I} \qquad \text{I} \quad \text{IV}_6^4 \quad \text{V}_6 \quad \text{I}$$

6. Categories - large forms

A = *fa*; find *do* (E)

A. Scales

1. Construct scale on E

- discover the need for four sharps to fit the tetrachord pattern

d'	E
t	D#
l	C#
s	B
f	A
m	G#
r	F#
d	E

- sing the E major scale in absolutes

B. Triads, Chords, and Inversions

TRIADS drill: Review what makes a triad major or minor

1. Cherubini No. 2

- sing in canon
- pull out I triad
- review "inversions" d-m-s; m-s-d'; s-d'-m'
  1- 3-5; 3 -5-1; 5- 1-3
- sing I V_6 I progression

2. New: Cherubini Canon No. 1 (See page 123)

- read rhythm
- read in *solfa*
- find I chord
- focus on 3rd phrase - measure 2
- figure out chord: there is another third on top of the triad
- what makes a "7" chord?

C. Prepare for Listening

3. Beethoven

- sing melody
- sing bass part
- label chords:

Phrase 1	I					—————— IV
Phrase 2	V_7	I	vi	IV	V_7	I

- sing roots of chords while melody played:

d —————					f
s_1	d	l_1	f_1	s_1	d

4. Listen to recording

- fill out column one of the listening chart (See page 127)

D. Compound Meter

5. Meter of the Beethoven? $\left(^6_8\right)$

- what does this really mean?
- sing and conduct - "I's The B'y"
- sing and conduct - "Rocky Mountain"
  - how are they the same? Both move in 2s
  - how are they different? (In "Rocky Mountain" the subdivisions are in 2s; in Beethoven the subdivisions are in 3s)
  - subdivision of the conducting beat: ♫ simple meter ♫♪ compound meter

* Vocabulary terms: simple meter - subdivision of beat ♪♪ 2s, compound meter - subdivision of beat ♪♪♪ 3s

E. Game

5. Categories - performing artists

A = *ti*; find *do* (B♭)

1. Tone/Absolute Ladder

- sing scale in *solfa* from tone ladder
- compare *solfa* with absolute ladder
- derive key signature for B♭
  - what is wrong with E? (too high)
  - what is needed (a lower note; E♭)

2. Cherubini No. 2

- sing with rhythm syllables
- sing with solfa
- sing as three-voice canon
- review V_7 chord
- describe 7-chords

3. New Song: "Fie, Nay Prithee, John" (See page 124)

- rote-note process
- discuss text
- find 7-chords
- label them

4. Beethoven No. 6 Finale—Listening

- sing theme in *solfa*
- sing bass line in *solfa*
- sing two parts together
- listen to discover form (use listening charts)

5. $\frac{6}{8}$ Meter Review

- sing and conduct "Yankee Doodle"
  - how is it moving? (2s)
  - clap an ostinato of eighths
  - how are the eighths moving? (2s) ♫
  * Vocabulary: simple meter
- sing and conduct "I's The B'y"
  - how is it moving? (2s)

- clap an ostinato of eighths
  - how are the eighths moving? (3s) ♪♪♪
  * Vocabulary: compound meter
- Detective Game: Is this simple or compound meter? Teacher sings as students tap an ostinato of *ti*'s to determine whether the beat subdivisions are in 2s (simple meter) or 3s (compound meter)

Whistle, Daughter, Whistle	The Ryans and the Pitmans
Twinkle, Twinkle Little Star	The Irish Washerwoman
Alabama Gal	The Noble Duke of York

6. Question and Answer Phrases

- sing a Questions phrase (readiness for Q-A phrases)

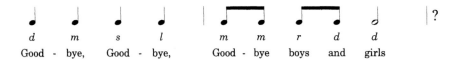

| d | m | s | l | m | m | r | d | d | ? |
| Good - | bye, | Good - | bye, | Good - | bye | boys | and | girls | |

- students answer, ending on do

A = *ti*; find *do* (B♭)

1. Review key of B♭

- sing scale
- sing *solfa*
- sing absolutes
- construct scale

2. Cherubini Canon No. 2

- sing in *solfa*
- 3-parts in canon
- identify the broken V_7 chord
- describe 7-chords - show on handstaff

3. "Fie, Nay Prithee, John"

- review - sing from memory
- how to locate "7" chords: line-line-line-line or space-space-space-space
- find the 7 chords in this song (last phrase)
- circle and name all. Write chord numbers in music
- sing as a 3-part canon

4. Beethoven Symphony No. 6 - *The Pastorale*

- review the form (Rondo)
- sing melody; bass line
- listen to first three theme statements to determine what instruments are playing the theme?
- enter information on listening guide

5. Is the Beethoven in Compound ♪♪♪ or Simple meter ♪♪?

- Compound? How can you tell?
- How about these pieces?
    "Rocky Mountain" (simple, duple meter)

"Down in the Valley" (compound triple meter)
"Lavender's Blue" (simple triple meter)

HOMEWORK: Memorize "Fie, Nay Prithee John" *solfa* and text

MOUNT ROYAL CONSERVATORY—LESSON 19

A = *di* (half step lower to *do*) - A♭

1. **Bars and Discs for key of A♭:**

d'	A♭
t	G
l	F
s	E♭
f	D♭
m	C
r	B♭
d	A♭

- thirds drill beginning on A♭
- Triads beginning on A♭

2. **Fie, Nay Prithee, John**

- sing in *solfa*
- isolate 7 chords
- discuss intervals - 4th, 5ths, 6ths
- discover all the 6ths in this song
- discover principal: if the 3rd is major its inversion (the 6th) is minor. If the 3rd is minor, its inversion (the 6th) is major
- sing with text as a 3-voice canon

3. **Pastorale—Beethoven**

- listen to second entrance of the theme. It is hidden in scale passages. Sing bass part with this theme statement.
- enter instrumentation on listening chart

4. **New Song: "He Shall Feed His Flock,"** from the *Messiah*, by George Frederic Handel (in quadruple, compound meter, $\frac{12}{8}$)

5. Review Simple and Compound meters

- Conduct the following songs in simple and compound meters while singing.

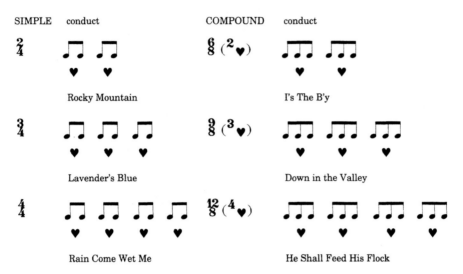

HOMEWORK: Compose a 4-phrase rhythm composition in a compound meter, in AABA form.

CONCLUSION

These nineteen lessons have introduced the students to:

- simple and compound meters and their conducting patterns
- most common rhythm patterns
- pentatonic and diatonic major and minor scales
- intervals of major and minor seconds and thirds
- tonic, subdominant, and dominant chords in root position and in inversion
- implied harmonies
- basic tempo and dynamics terminology
- simple forms
- key signatures and scale construction

The students have sung in unison, in two and in three parts.

They have increased their solfa ability.
They have composed rhythmic and melodic variations.
They have listened to music for specific purposes.
They have experienced variation form and rondo form.
They have identified instruments in listening examples.
They have notated simple rhythmic and melodic examples.
They have had some experience in each class with music reading.
They have acquired a basic musical vocabulary.

In a word, these students are now ready to embark on a comprehensive curriculum in music.

Chapter 3

What Shall We Teach Once a Common Musical Vocabulary Is in Place?

Let us stop the teachers superstition according to which only some diluted art-substitute is suitable for teaching purposes.[1]

A hundred lifetimes would not be enough to get to know all the good music that exists. Nevertheless, you must get to know all significant works of all significant masters. Do not propagate bad works; on the contrary, fight against them with might and main.[2]

Kodály's writings repeatedly emphasized that the principle aim of music education in the schools must be:

…to make the masterpieces of world literature public property, to convey them to people of every kind and rank.…[3]

Somehow over the years and in many places, including even in some schools in Hungary, this important goal has been subverted. The desired outcome envisioned by Kodály of a literate and knowledgeable musical public, supportive of the arts, and thoroughly conversant with the great music of the western world, has to some extent become lost in the pursuit of musical literacy in its narrowest sense. In schools, musical reading and writing have become ends rather than means. At worst, there is an attitude that the music through which literacy is achieved is immaterial. Technical facility has been deemed more important than the development of musical taste.

One is compelled to ask "literacy for what?" If musical knowledge and values are not being imparted at the same time that skills necessary for reading and writing music are being developed, of what possible use are those skills? Literacy has value to the general population only to the extent that it can open ears and minds to music

---

[1] Zoltan Kodály, *Selected Writings*, p. 122.

[2] Zoltan Kodály, *Selected Writings*, p. 188.

[3] Zoltan Kodály, *Selected Writings*, p. 160.

that might otherwise be beyond understanding and enjoyment. Kodály believed that if the world of serious music was to survive, the schools would have to prepare students in such a way that they would love that serious music. Merely learning to sight sing is not sufficient preparation for this. At every point during the continuum of music education, music used for teaching must be of the highest quality, whether that music is folk or composed; and at some point the balance must shift from folk music to composed music if Kodály's desire to "make the masterpieces of world literature public property" is ever to be realized.

THE HUNGARIAN MODEL

In an attempt to follow Kodály's lead, the authors of the Hungarian Singing School textbooks, *Enek Zene,*[4] begin introducing music of serious composers by the third grade. The earliest examples are folk song arrangements by well-known Hungarian composers—Kodály, Bartok, Bardos, Szönyi, and others. In fourth grade the first listening examples are included. These increase in number and complexity grade by grade through the eighth-grade text, the last of the series. While in the grade-four book there are many folk songs and few examples of composed music, by the eighth grade folk songs are very few in number. The musical material consists primarily of art music examples to sing, to analyze and hear, ranging from Josquin des Prez to Shostakovich. Further, students in these schools in Hungary generally deal with this music knowledgeably and musically. They perform, analyze, listen to, and create within the framework of the masterworks that are the core of their curriculum.

IMPLICATIONS FOR MUSIC PROGRAMS
IN NORTH AMERICA

In Hungary there appears to be an unbroken line from kindergarten through eighth grade, in which skill is layered carefully upon skill, understanding upon understanding, and value upon value. In most North American schools the process breaks down somewhere around fourth grade. The reasons for this are easy enough to discern.

First, in the Hungarian schools under discussion here,[5] music is taught daily. More can be accomplished and far less review and repetition are necessary than in the more usual twice-weekly North American situation. Second, music teacher training is far more rigorous in Hungary than in any institution in North America. Five years of the highest level conservatory training are required as the entry level to teaching positions in the Singing Music Schools. Teachers must excel as performers even to be admitted to teacher training programs, and their immersion in musicianship and literature classes is intense throughout the five years. There is a firm commitment to the

---

[4] *Enek Zene*, Nemesszeghy, Márta and Szábo, Helga, Tankönykiadó, Budapest, 1968.

[5] The *Enek Zene Iskola* are 160 public elementary schools in which music is treated as a major subject and scheduled for 45 minutes daily for at least four days a week.

principle that to teach a subject well, even at the most elemental level, it is necessary to know it thoroughly at the highest levels.

This is vastly different from teacher training programs in North America, which are largely dedicated to the notion that one doesn't really need to know much more than the children; one simply needs to know how to teach. Method replaces substance in many Faculties of Education.

In spite of this there are many fine musicians teaching music in North American schools. They have often been shortchanged in their college or university years, but few groups seem so determined to do the job right. At a time when summer courses are waning in most other fields, music teachers continue to flock to summer workshops to upgrade skills and to seek further knowledge. The picture is far from hopeless.

A third reason for this breakdown in the continuity of music education is that there are books in the Hungarian schools— not commercial series meant to be all things to all people, as in North America— but carefully graded, full sequential texts, written by some of the best musicians and music educators in Hungary.

There has to this point been no single book produced for English-speaking students that can begin to compare favorably with the *Enek Zene* texts. A number of attempts have been made at the lower grade levels, some with a degree of success. Nothing of note has been produced for more advanced classes. Part of the blame for this must be laid at the door of publishers, who do not generally view such a text as commercially viable.

In the face of these difficulties, is it possible to achieve the outcomes Kodály envisioned? Most certainly yes. A good teacher, who is also a good musician, and who teaches using only the best music, can in two years instill in students indelibly for life a love of music supported by knowledge about music.[6] This was Kodály's aim.

ORGANIZING A CURRICULAR FRAMEWORK
FOR TEACHING AND LEARNING

If we accept as valid the notion that the quality of the music we use for teaching is all important, the first step in developing a curriculum must logically involve making choices from the vast array of music available to us. What music should be used? There is no hard and fast rule for selecting music for teaching. However, there are some general guidelines:

1. Choose music of composers universally accepted as great. Do not use an example by Offenbach or Dukas when one by Beethoven or Bach is available.
2. Use the genuine masterworks of those great composers. Even the greatest have created some works of less significance, of less genius than others. The frequently performed repertory of concert halls and symphony orchestras is per-

---

[6] Music teachers who doubt the veracity of this statement should simply ask themselves why they chose music as a career. In most instances it was the influence of a single dynamic teacher. In the author's case it happened in one year, in a seventh-grade general music class in a little country school.

formed often for a reason. Most of it is memorable music. Students should be prepared for this repertory, rather than taught through works they will likely never hear outside the classroom.

3. Choose music from every period and style. There is music suitable for teaching ranging from Gregorian chant to twentieth-century polytonality and atonality.
4. Select a variety of musical forms and genres. Do not limit your teaching to symphonies and program music.
5. Vary the instrumentation choices. There should be representative examples of large ensembles, small ensembles, and solo performances of instrumental and vocal music. Symphony orchestras, wind ensembles, early music groups, opera ensembles, string quartets, and electroacoustic media are just some of the possibilities. To the extent that it is possible, all the ways that people make serious music should be included.

Most music teachers can recall one, two, or three years spent in music history classes at the university level in which the teaching began with early music and proceeded ploddingly through the centuries, never quite getting past 1910. This kind of survey teaching leaves the student with a mass of miscellaneous information, a smattering of facts and very little in-depth knowledge of music itself.

Chronological order is not necessarily the best order for teaching; and a names/dates and fact-based approach is most certainly not the way to impart musical values. Another way is clearly needed. The most melodic, singable music is the music of Mozart and Haydn. This is the easiest point from which to embark on any journey into music. To students reared on a diet of folksongs, the flowing melodies, regular meters and simple forms of this period are an easy step into the world of art music.

From music of the classical style, the curriculum could move gradually back in time to the Baroque and Renaissance and forward to the Romantic and Impressionistic. Early music and twentieth-century music are the least accessible to most people and are best approached after a considerable level of musical sophistication has been achieved.

This sequence of study has been used for many years and with great success in the schools in Hungary:

1. Classical
2. Baroque/Romantic
3. Renaissance/Impressionist
4. Early Music/20th Century Music

This is not to imply that the Classical period is completed first. It is only begun first. The study of works in the Classical style, once begun, is continued throughout the grades. More complex works are studied and are studied in greater depth as students progress. The sequence involves only beginning points. There are no ending points. It might be more accurately shown as:

Viennese Classical _____⟶
Baroque _____⟶
Romantic _____⟶
Renaissance _____⟶
Impressionists _____⟶
Early Music _____⟶
20th Century Music _____⟶

What can be taught from this music? In a word: everything. There is no aspect of musical learning that cannot be uncovered through a systematic study of masterworks. Returning to the twelfth grade student described in Chapter 1, all ten of the outcomes listed in that description can be achieved through such study.

All basic musical behaviors can be involved: performing, listening, analyzing, and creating. All elements of music can be explored: duration (beat, rhythm, meter), pitch movements (melody), simultaneous sounds (harmony), form, tempo, timbre, and dynamics. All the ways in which students experience music can be utilized: singing, playing instruments, listening, moving, reading, writing, improvising and composing.

How is this different from most teaching practice today? School curricula tend to be comprised of hierarchies of skills and concepts, and are arranged from simplest to most complex, which are then somewhat arbitrarily divided into grade levels. Music is suggested through which to teach each new skill. Much time is spent by curriculum committees trying to find the best songs through which to teach ♩♪ or low *la*. At the primary levels this approach has some validity. If basic literacy skills are to be developed they must be approached systematically in a manner congruent with child developmental characteristics and with what is known about how children learn. With upper grade students who have attained some level of functional music literacy, such an approach is counterproductive. To look through art music for a good example of, for instance, the harmonic minor scale, is simply backward. In any core of well-chosen art music, the harmonic minor scale will appear some place. When it appears it can be studied.

In simplest terms, the music must come first. When the music is well chosen, everything we want to teach may be found in it. Dobsay states:

I have become increasingly convinced that the direction of music teaching can best be determined by the inner logic of the music itself.[7]

THE PEDAGOGICAL CYCLE

All who have ever used the Kodály approach are probably aware of the teaching/learning cycle, in which, for each new learning students are first prepared through rote singing experiences over a period of time, next made consciously aware of the new

---

[7] Ibid, p. 10.

rhythmic or melodic figure (given its *solfa* or rhythmic syllable, shown its relative place on the staff or its notation), then undergo a lengthy period of learning reinforcement through reading and notating previously learned and new songs, and finally have their learning assessed through prima vista reading examples and through improvising and composing using the new rhythmic figure or melodic turn. This is listed somewhat simplistically as: prepare, present, and practice. This cycle is repeated for every new tonal pattern, each new rhythmic figure, throughout the lower grades.

The pedagogical process does not change when we approach the teaching of art music. The emphasis merely shifts. In constructing a long-range plan for a series of listening lessons, rather than preparing students for high *do* or ♪ ♩ ♪ , the teacher must now analyze the music thoroughly to determine what the students need to know in order to listen to it with understanding. He or she must then prepare the students for these new learnings.

The "make conscious" stage might be viewed as the first time the students actually listen to the work. The music is then reinforced through repeated listening, each with a specific focus.

Assessment may take many forms. At a simple level, students might compose a short work incorporating some techniques learned through the particular composition. This will, however, assess only superficial knowledge. The most valuable outcome of such teaching lies in the development of musical taste and long-term acquisition of musical values. These are not qualities easy to assess.

Constructing a Long-Range Listening Strategy

A listening strategy is a series of relatively short teaching segments that take place over many lessons. It includes all the preparation activities and states the purpose of each as related to the chosen composition, as well as the listening activities themselves, with a clearly delineated focus for each. To construct a listening strategy:

1. Pick a work you enjoy. If it is a long work, choose one part of it. Notate the part you plan to use in a singable key.
2. Listen to the work many times. Know it well.
3. Ask yourself:
   - What do students need to know to listen to this with understanding?
   - What is its form?
   - What is its harmonic structure?
   - What compositional devices are used? (augmentation, diminution, canonic entrances, rhythmic or metric variation, key shifts, etc.)
   - How much of this can I teach through singing, before we listen? Which aspects should I teach through the music itself?
4. Choose the main aspect on which you wish to focus your teaching of this work. Construct a listening chart for students to complete gradually, some parts after

each listening, so that at the end of the listening cycle they will have a written guide for future reference.

The number of lessons in such a series is somewhat arbitrary and depends to a great extent on the complexity of the work to be studied. However, four to six lessons might be spent in preparation activities before first hearing the work. After that, a recording of the composition might be played in three successive lessons, each with a different specific listening purpose.

At this point the work could be put aside for a few weeks, before returning to it to listen again, focusing on still another aspect.[8] Later in the year, and even in the following year, it may be revisited. Other performances may be listened to and compared with the familiar one. Generalizations about period and style may also be drawn. If only one section of the work has been studied, other sections may be introduced. The work may be compared with other works by the same composer or in the same style; or it may be compared with works of other periods.

The approach suggested here is very different from the ones commonly in use in the schools. The focus is on the music, throughout. It is better to study two works a year in this kind of depth than to listen to ten works superficially, because this analytical approach makes generalization possible. The student who has studied Mozart's Symphony No. 40 in G Minor, who knows the work thoroughly, can sing its themes, follow its forms and its harmonic progressions and key changes, can then listen with much greater understanding to all Mozart and Haydn symphonies. He or she is able to transfer the knowledge acquired and, even more importantly, the appreciation that goes with the knowledge to other works in the same style and period.

SINGING AS THE BASIS FOR LISTENING

In a Kodály approach, *listen* is an action verb; and as with all other aspects of Kodály practice, listening is approached first through singing. The step from singing beautiful folk songs to singing the music of Mozart or Mendelssohn is a small one; and singing such music can produce a more lasting affection for it than mere hearing ever can. Discs and tapes are not the only way to become familiar with great music. They are not the best way. They are useful as an intermediary step between singing and concert attendance. Through singing, students take knowledge and understanding to the listening experience, whether it is recorded or live.

This is only possible if the student knows and can sing the themes he or she is going to hear, has thought about the implied harmonic construction, and has applied some of the compositional techniques. When the student listens it is not to hear how the music goes, but rather to hear how Beethoven resolved the melodic question, how

---

[8] Although I cannot quote empirical research to prove the point, many years of classroom work have led me to believe that giving a composition a rest is a more effective way of making students want to hear it than simply repeated listening to it lesson after lesson. If it has not been heard for two or three weeks, students appear to bring fresher minds to the task and to enjoy the listening more.

Mozart used a transition from minor to major to create interest, how Bach used rhythmic augmentation in the last statement of a fugue tune, or how Bernstein used $\frac{7}{8}$ meter to create an interesting effect.

LEVELS OF MUSIC LISTENING

There are many levels of music listening. There is being in the presence of sound: elevator music, music in shopping malls, and music over the telephone when one is put on hold. These may be heard, but are seldom listened to. Then there is listening vaguely to something we like while doing something else. We may be listening but only with a small part of our minds.

There is quiet and attentive listening to music, in a concert hall, for example, where our attention is, or at least appears to be, on the music. And there is the kind of knowledgeable listening in which minds and emotions are fully engaged; in which we anticipate what is going to happen next, and are capable of making judgments about the level of the performance.

It is this last kind of listening toward which we should be directing our students. Only this level requires education.

A SUGGESTED CURRICULUM BASED ON SELECTED WORKS, COMPOSERS, PERIODS, STYLES, FORMS, AND ENSEMBLES

Any choices of composers' works must, by definition, leave other composers, other works, unchosen. This is not intended to imply that some of these unchosen composers are less worthy of study. The composers and works offered here have been selected because they are typical of particular periods, styles, forms, and compositional techniques. Students should be able to extrapolate the understandings and knowledge acquired through study of these works to other compositions and composers of the same periods and styles. The composers and periods selected for inclusion in this admittedly incomplete curriculum are:

Baroque	Bach, Handel
Classical	Mozart, Haydn, Beethoven
Romantic	Schubert, Brahms
Impressionist	Debussy
20th century	Stravinsky

In choosing specific forms for study an attempt was made to select those that are most basic and those from which others evolved: song form, minuet and trio, theme and variation, rondo, fugue, ritornello, dance forms, passacaglia, and sonata. The ensemble choices include vocal and instrumental, large ensembles, small ensembles, and solo works.

Music theory is incorporated in the teaching segments. A systematic study of intervals, scales, chords, and chord progressions is developed through the works offered for study.

CONCLUSION

The course of study offered on the following pages is extensive but by no means complete. It may be extended to infinity from any point. There is no end to the study of music; there are are only beginnings.

Chapter 4

First Experiences in Directed Listening

MUSIC OF THE CLASSICAL PERIOD

The word "Classical" has come to be used popularly to mean any and all serious music. It is used here, however, to refer specifically to music composed between 1750 and 1820 in a particular style. The best known composers in this style were Franz Joseph Haydn (1732–1809), Wolfgang Amadeus Mozart (1756–91) and Ludwig van Beethoven (1770–1827).

Music in this style tends to be homophonic (a single melody line supported by accompaniment) and highly melodic. Its folk-like tunes are both memorable and easy to sing. Forms are balanced and symmetrical, with 4-measure phrases often employing question and answer patterns. Harmonies are predominantly tonic (I), subdominant (IV), and dominant (V), and cadences are generally either plagel (IV-I), authentic (V-I), or deceptive (V-vi). Meter is very regular but there is considerable rhythmic variety.

One of the major innovations of this period was in the area of dynamics. While composers of earlier periods tended to maintain a single dynamic level throughout a movement, composers in the classical style often employed the whole range of dynamic possibilities within sections. They used both gradual and sudden dynamic changes in their works. No doubt this was in some part due to the increased use of the piano, invented in the early 1700s. Its predecessor, the harpsichord, did not have the capability for subtle dynamic changes. The gradual crescendo and decrescendo were new ideas in the 1770s, when Mozart was composing for the fortepiano.

The classical orchestra was a very small one by twentieth-century standards. It could number as few as twenty-five instruments, and commonly consisted of:

Strings:	violins, violas, cellos, double basses
Woodwinds:	2 flutes, 2 oboes, 2 clarinets, 2 bassoons
Brass:	2 trumpets, 2 French horns[1]
Percussion:	2 timpani

Popular large forms were symphonies, concertos, and string quartets. These were three or four movement forms defined by meter and tempo: fast, slow, moderate 3/4, fast. The third movement, usually a minuet in symphonies, was omitted in concertos. Within movements themes were often sharply contrasting in character.

The Historic Setting

Vienna was the center of the musical universe during this period, and the three musical giants of classicism, Haydn, Mozart, and Beethoven, all spent a significant part of their lives in that city. It was a period of strife encompassing the French Revolution, the American Revolution, and the Napoleonic Wars. There was great unrest politically, signalling the demise of the aristocracy, a sharp reduction in the powers of the Church and the rise of the middle class. The lives and careers of these three composers were a microcosm of the social changes surrounding them.

Haydn spent most of his life in the employ of an aristocrat, Nicholas Eszterházy, ostensibly as a court composer, but actually as little better than a servant. Mozart, born just twenty-four years after Haydn, rejected the role of servant, turning his back on positions that might have given him financial security, to write for a more public forum. He enjoyed considerable financial and artistic success in Vienna and Prague, but died young and very nearly destitute.

Beethoven, arriving on the scene only marginally later, was able throughout his life to support himself as an independent musician. The day of the "common man" had arrived.

What Do Students Need to Know to Approach Music of This Period?

If instruments of the orchestra have been studied previously and can be identified visually and aurally, the classical orchestra can be discovered through listening. Which instruments found in the twentieth-century orchestra are not present? Obviously the low brass and many percussion instruments.

The piano, so beloved by Mozart and Beethoven, is deserving of some attention in the classroom. The twentieth-century grand piano found in concert halls should be compared in size and sound to the fortepiano of Mozart's day and to its predecessor,

---

[1] Trombones existed, but were used only rarely in orchestral works.

the harpsichord. All should be compared to the harp, among the oldest of all instruments, and the one that, turned on its side and attached to plucking or hammering devices, is the ancestor of all stringed keyboard instruments.

Piano

The beginning point for this study should probably be the piano, since students will already be familiar with its sound, and since there will likely be one in the school. If the piano should happen to be a grand, students can observe the action of the hammers hitting the strings to produce sound, and can experiment with changing that sound by touching the strings (stopping the vibration) or by plucking them gently (changing the quality of the sound).

An upright piano can be used in the same way if the front panel is easily removable and replaceable. The same generalizations that were drawn about orchestral instruments should be drawn about the piano:

1. The metal of the strings, the wood of the hammers and the felt of the dampers all affect the quality of the sound.
2. The playing mode affects the dynamic level. (Strike the key harder, the sound is louder. Press it more lightly, the sound is softer.)
3. The length and the thickness of the strings determines how high or low the pitch is.
4. The wooden box amplifies the sound.

From this exploratory lesson the teacher might move to a recorded example, Mozart's Variations on "Ah, Vous dirai-je, Maman" ("Twinkle, Twinkle Little Star"). This work is particularly useful because the tune is already familiar and because recordings exist of both piano and harpsichord performances. Listening first to a bit of the piano recording, the teacher might then shift to the harpsichord one: "Is the instrument the same or different?" "How is the sound different?" "Does it remind you of any of the sounds we produced when we experimented with the piano?" (The plucked sound.) At this point, pictures of harpsichords should be shown, and some basic information given.

Harpsichord

The harpsichord was a common stringed keyboard instrument from the sixteenth to the eighteenth century. Harpsichord strings are plucked by quills rather than struck by hammers, as the piano is. One cannot change the dynamic level by touch as one can on the piano. It does not have the dramatic and expressive qualities of the piano, but it has a sharp, clear sound that makes it possible to hear inner and lower voices more distinctly.

If possible the lessons on stringed instruments should include a field trip to see a collection; they exist in many cities. One of the finest is in the Smithsonian Institute in Washington, D.C. Many community music schools and university music departments also own harpsichords, clavichords, and fortepianos. The teacher might try to arrange a visit to see and hear them, or to have the class attend a concert featuring one of these instruments.

RONDO FORM

LISTENING STRATEGY 1

Mozart, Horn Concerto No. 4 in Eb Major, K. 495 (III. Rondo)

Rondo is one of the easiest forms with which to begin a listening program because of its thematic repetition. Rondos consist of one main tune alternating with a series of other tunes. The usual pattern is A B A C A D A or A B A C A B A. This is generally followed by a coda, a concluding statement with a feeling of finality, that lets the listener know the movement is ending.

In preparing to listen to this rondo students should have experience with compound meter, I and V chords, question and answer phrases and rondo form.

Compound Meter

In rote singing 6/8 is as natural to students as breathing. It is, after all the meter of the English language. On this rote level, the easiest way to distinguish between 2/4 or 4/4 and 6/8 is through movement. The former are stepping meters, while the latter is a skipping meter. It is strongly recommended that through a series of folk dances such as "Captain Jinks" (6/8) and "Old Brass Wagon"[2] (2/4) the physical feeling of simple and compound meters be brought to students. The reading and writing of 6/8 will be easier if this movement experience has preceded it.

---

[2] See *120 Singing Games & Dances*, Choksy and Brummitt, Prentice Hall.

Procedure

YANKEE DOODLE

Sing "Yankee Doodle." Conduct it as you sing.

Question: *How is it moving?* (in 2s)

Clap an ostinato of ♪'s as you sing.

Question: *How many ♪'s did you clap over each conducting beat?* (2, ♫)

Conclusion: In "Yankee Doodle," the ♪'s move in twos over the beat.

BONAVIST HARBOUR

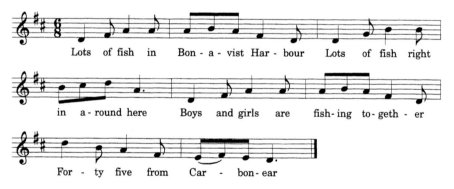

Sing "Bonavist Harbour." Conduct as you sing.

Question: *How is it moving?* (in 2s)

Clap an ostinato of ♪'s as you sing "Bonavist Harbour."

Question: *How many ti's did you clap over each conducting beat?* (3, ♪♪♪)

Conclusion: In "Bonavist Harbour," the ♪'s move in 3s over the conducting beat.

This experience should be extended by singing other 2/4 and 6/8 songs, conducting them in 2s and clapping the ♪'s to discover whether they are moving in 2s ♫, or 3s ♪♪♪.

Vocabulary Terms:

- simple meter
- compound meter

Concept Inference

In simple meters the subdivision of the conducting beat is in 2s; in compound meters, the subdivisions of the conducting beat is in 3s. This generalization will hold true for all simple and all compound meters.

These activities should be followed by examination of the notation of 6/8 songs. Students will discover that the meter sign refers, not to the conducting beat, ♩. but to the beat subdivisions, ♪.

It will probably be helpful at this point to practice basic 6/8 rhythmic combinations, using a chart on the board:

The dotted line is meant to show the symmetry of the meter. Rarely does a rhythmic figure carry across that imaginary line, particularly in eighteenth-century music. Students may practice saying the chart in *ta*'s (♩), *ti*'s (♪), and *tam*'s (♩.) as the teacher indicates the line. When the rhythms are flowing well the teacher may shift from one line to another at the dotted line. In this way most common 6/8 rhythm patterns can be practiced.

Harmony: The I and V Chords in Major

Students should be able to feel simple tonic-dominant harmonic implications in melody and to sing the roots of these chords, as a second part, with a melody, as described in Chapter 1. We are now ready to add chords to these roots. All the songs suggested here must, of course, be well known to the students before attempting these activities.

d   m   s
Lots of fish in

The teacher should divide the class into three sections. Following the text, one section sings "lots" and holds the note, the other two sing "of" and "fish." They then repeat the activity using *solfa* syllables: *do, mi, so.*

> Questions: *What do we call this kind of sound? (Chord, Triad). How did we make the chord? If* do *is counted as the first step in the chord, counting up the scale, what are* mi *and* so*? (3 and 5.)*

> Conclusion: *Do-mi-so* is a chord. It is called the I chord or the tonic chord, because do is the first degree of the scale. Many pieces end with this chord.

Sing "I's the By." Again, the class should be divided into three sections. This time, the notes to be held are on "takes 'em home" *(so, ti, re.)*

> Question: *What is the lowest note, the root of this chord?* (so). *What degree of the scale is* so*? (5th, V). If we count* so *as the first step in this chord, moving up the scale, what are* ti *and* re*? (3 and 5.)*

> Conclusion: *so-ti-re* is a chord. It is called the V chord or dominant chord.

Concept Inference

A chord may be built on any degree of the scale by singing the 3rd and 5th steps over the root. Chords are named for the degree of the scale occupied by the root.

Students should practice singing thirds and triads until they are easy to perform from memory.

Later, students learn about major (big) thirds and minor (little) thirds. They classify chords as of major or minor character and use uppercase (major) and lowercase (minor) Roman numerals when labeling them:

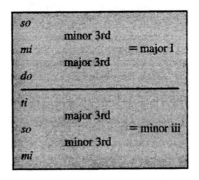

Concept Inference

The major or minor quality of a chord is determined by the interval between 1 and 3. If that 3rd is major the chord is major. If that third is minor the chord is minor.

Diminished and augmented triads may be studied later, when the musical material requires them.

Question and Answer Phrases

Some phrases have a feeling of finality:

ROCKY MOUNTAIN

While others feel incomplete; as if more must follow:

The incomplete phrase is a question phrase, the complete one an answer phrase.

BEETHOVEN, SYMPHONY NO. 9,
FOURTH MOVEMENT

Most questions end on a note of the V or V₇ chord (*so, ti, re* or *fa*) and most answer phrases end on *do*. Pull question phrases out of folk songs the students know. Sing the question phrase and stop.

> Question: *Does that sound complete? What is needed to complete it? (Students sing the phrase that completes the music.)*

> Concept Inference: A phrase that sounds incomplete is a question phrase and a phrase that balances and completes the musical idea is an answer phrase.

> The teacher may reinforce this by:
> *Locate question and answer phrases in familiar songs. Keep a list of question-phrase ending notes. What have we found most frequently as the final notes in question phrases?* (re, so, ti). Conclusion: These are the notes of the V chord.

> Concept Inference: *The most common question-phrase resting point (cadence) is on a note of the V chord.* The teacher may reinforce this by singing melodic question phrases to which students improvise answer phrases.

Rondo Form

Students should have been analyzing songs as they learn them, placing the letters *a, b,* and *c,* beside the notation to show which phrases are the same, which different, and which similar. It is suggested that they use lowercase letters for this exercise so that later, sections of larger forms may be diagrammed with uppercase letters A, B, C, and so on. It is also suggested that, rather than using primes (a¹) or v's for variant (aᵛ), when the first *a* is a musical question and the second *a* an answer, this be shown simply as *a?* and *a!* While this technique is not the one in use in formal analysis it has the advantage of being specific. If the second a or b really is a variant rather than an answer, then a¹ or aᵛ may be used.

In transferring this learning to rondo form, rhythmic improvisation or composition may be used.

Procedure: *Compose a two measure phrase in* ⁶⁄₈*. Notate it. Get together in groups of four. Decide who in your group will be "a," who "b," who "c," and who "d." Your form is a-b-a-c-a-d-a. This is called rondo form, because the "a" keeps coming around again. Practice performing your rondo. You have five minutes.*

With rondo form, ⁶⁄₈ meter, and I-V harmonies in place the students are now ready to begin to study the Mozart concerto for which we have been preparing.

Preparing for the First Listening Lesson

The next lessons are designed to make students familiar with some aspects of the work they are going to hear before they actually listen to it. This is so that when they listen even for the first time they will take knowledge and understanding to that listening. The rhythm of the "A" theme may be placed on the board and used as a rhythm-erase game:

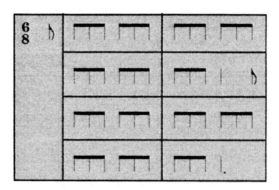

Question: *What is the form of this rhythm? (a-b-a-b)*

Once the example has been read aloud smoothly and correctly, the students are instructed to memorize it. A minute or so of quiet time should be allowed for memorization. After this the teacher erases the *a* phrases and the class reads the whole, including the missing phrases. Then the teacher erases the *b* phrases and the exercise is repeated. By this time even students who have difficulty with memorization know this four phrase rhythm. A paper should now be distributed on which the students notate the rhythm they have memorized. In the next class period the students may be given the melody. This may be shown either as stem and solfa notation, which they can later place on staff, or it may be given initially as staff notation. If the latter, it should be notated in an easily singable key. In the case of this composition, no change of key is necessary; the range is comfortable in E^b as originally notated.

The students sing the theme in *solfa*, analyze the form again, now that the melody has been added, and memorize the tune. They may well perceive the form as two phrases at this point:

First Listening

The recording may now be played. It is a short movement (3:55 minutes) and may be played in its entirety. Students will be listening to discover:

How many times does this theme occur? (8)
If we call the first theme "A," what is the complete form?
(A-A-B—A-A-C—A-A-B-A and ending with bits of A.)

A listening chart could be given to the students on which they can enter this information. This Listening Chart will be used in many subsequent lessons.

Listening Chart

Work: _____

Composer: _____   Dates: _____

Style: _____

Form	Instruments	Dynamics	Tempo	Maj/min	Other

Students will hear that the last theme statement is somewhat different from the other "A" statements and clearly forecasts the end of the movement. The word *coda* may be taught for this kind of closing section and should be entered in the listening chart in the last space under "form."

Second Listening

In another class period attention should be directed to the instrumentation of this work. The orchestra of the period should be reviewed and discussed, and the students should be asked if they recall what the solo instrument in this concerto was (French horn). The word *tutti* may be taught as a way of indicating full orchestra.

As the recording is played, students should indicate on their charts whether the themes are being played by the French horn or by the full orchestra. The term *concerto* may be taught to mean a three-movement work featuring a solo instrument (or instruments) accompanied by orchestra.

Third Listening

Before the third listening experience the class should learn the "B" theme:

This may be given, like the "A" theme, in either stem and *solfa* or in staff notation. The focus of the third listening is on the dynamics used throughout the movement. Students should be encouraged to use traditional dynamic markings, *f, mf, mp,* and *p* as well as *crescendo* and *decrescendo* markings to indicate what they hear within each theme statement. It is helpful to listen to the opening and decide as a class whether it is *mf* or *mp* or simply a moderate dynamic level. With the beginning listed in a uniform way throughout the class, later comparisons among answers will have more validity.

Fourth Listening

Only the "A" theme section in its first two statements will be played in this lesson, but it will be played twice. The objective is to determine how Mozart harmonized this theme.

Before listening the students should attempt to harmonize the melody by singing *do* and *so* as the teacher or a small group of students sing the melody. When the class has agreed on a likely harmonization they should mark it into the notation of the theme using I and V to indicate where they think the chord changes occur.

Now the recording is played and the students are encouraged to sing their *do-so* harmonization softly to determine whether Mozart's harmonization is the same as theirs.

Do your do's *and* so's *fit? (*Yes.*)*
*Is Mozart's bass line the same as ours? (*No.*)*
The harmonization you have marked is basically correct, but Mozart did not use only the roots of the I and V chords. Sometimes he used the 3rd or the 5th in his bass part.

At this point the class should be given the notation of the bass line to sing.

Is there any note in this bass line that is not in the I or V chord? (Only one, "C" in measure 4.) The "A" section is played once again and students sing Mozart's bass line softly as they listen.

Fifth Listening

At this listening students focus on tempo and use traditional tempo terminology to mark entries on their listening charts. The tempo of this movement is moderately fast or allegretto throughout. However in two places the tempo slows noticeably. The term ritardando should be taught for this kind of temporary slowing down.

Sixth Listening

The students listen to discover whether there is any place in the rondo where a shift occurs from major to minor. (The "C" statement). This is marked into their listening charts. At this time they could also be given opportunity to enter any additional comments they may have in the "other" column.

Concluding Activities

By this time students know this work well and some background information on Mozart and on the period in which Mozart lived might be interesting to them. It is useful to place the composer historically with respect to people or events the students may know about through their history classes. Mozart lived at the same time as George Washington and Thomas Jefferson. He was born just before General Wolfe fought the Battle of the Plains of Abraham and was a young man when the Quebec Act was passed, granting freedom of religion to Canadian Roman Catholics.

Biographies could be suggested, and the movie *Amadeus* might be recommended or made available to students, as well. While the latter is certainly highly fictionalized it nevertheless is an entertaining picture of the era, which contains much fine music, well performed.

Below is a guide for the teacher indicating what the listening chart should look like when completed. Some of the columns, tempo, and dynamics particularly may vary depending upon the performer, conductor, and ensemble; however the general outline is accurate.

Listening Chart

Work: Horn Concerto in E♭ Major, K. 495

Composer: Wolfgang Amadeus Mozart   **Dates: 1756–91**

Style: Viennese Classical

Form	Instruments	Dynamics	Tempo	Maj/min	Other
A	French horn	mf (moderately loud)	moderately fast	Major	I-V harmony
A	Tutti	f	same	Major	
B	Fr. horn	mf to mp to mf	same	Major	broken chords in second half
A	Fr. horn	mf	same	Major	
A	Tutti	f	same	Major	
C	Fr. horn	softer	ritardando	minor	
A	Fr. horn	p	\	Major	
A	Tutti	f	allegretto	Major	
B	Fr. horn	horn softer, orchestra louder	ritardando at end	Major	solo horn melody orchestra at end
A	Fr. horn/ orchestra	mf - f		Major	long chord V held; pause before coda
Coda	Fr. horn & orchestra			Major	bits of A theme. descending broken sequence chords. strong cadence

LISTENING STRATEGY 2

Haydn, Cello Concerto in D Major, Op.101; Third Movement, Rondo.

As a follow up to the rondo from the Mozart horn concerto, the rondo from this Haydn cello concerto is an easy step, requiring little additional preparation. The teaching pattern can be almost identical to that followed for the Mozart. The rhythm and meter could be isolated and dealt with first:

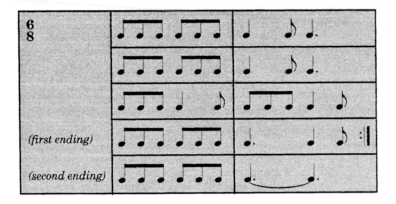

If the students have not previously encountered first and second endings they can be taught through this example. Before introducing the themes the teacher should draw students' attention to examples of repetition at higher and lower places in known songs and teach the term *sequence*:

When the "A" theme of this rondo is introduced, students should be asked to find the sequence. (The second phrase is a repeat of the first phrase, one step lower):

CELLO CONCERTO

First Listening

Diagram the form.

Second Listening

List the instrument(s) playing the themes at each statement.

Third Listening

Enter the dynamics on the listening charts.

Fourth Listening

Before the fourth listening it will be neceassary to extend students' knowledge of harmony to the subdominant (IV) chord.

LUMBERMAN'S ALPHABET

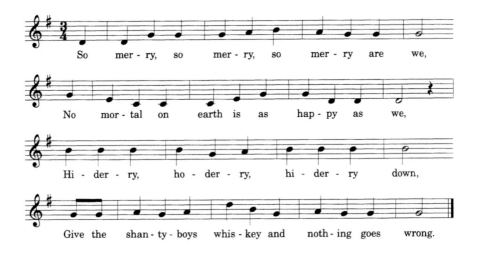

Procedure: Sing the song in *solfa*, following the notation.
Question: *Can you find any triads in this melody? Phrase 4, measure 2 (*so, mi, do*) and phrase 2, measures 1 & 2 (*fa, la, do*).*

The class should then be led to sing these as chords.

BONAVIST HARBOUR

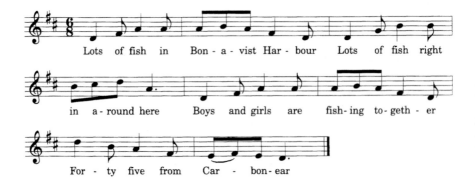

Procedure: Sing the song in *solfa*, following the notation.
Questions: *We found the I chord in the first phrase of this song. Can you find the IV chord in it? It may not have the root on the bottom. (Phrase 2, measure 1;* do, fa, la.*)*

The class should practice singing the two chords as they occur in "Bonavist Harbour":

s—l
m—f
d—d
I—IV$_6^4$

Conclusion: *We can turn a chord upside down. It is then in inversion. Any note of a chord may appear on the bottom. The notes of a chord may appear in any order.*

Examples of cadences should be developed with the class:

Procedure: *Beginning with s, m, d, how could we arrange the notes of the V chord so that they are easy to sing?*

s—s
m—r
d—t$_1$
I—V

Beginning with IV in the inversion in Bonavist Harbour, how could we move from IV to V to I?

l—s—s
f—r—m
d—t—d
IV—V—I

Students should then improvise a harmonization for the "A" theme of this rondo, singing the tonic, subdominant and dominant chord roots *do, fa,* and *so* with the melody. When they have done this, and marked the harmonization into their music, they are ready to listen.

Sing your harmony part softly as you listen. Does it fit? (Yes.)
Is the bass line by Haydn the same as the one you sang? (No.) Haydn used the I, IV, and V chords where you did, but he didn't always use the chord root in the bass.

The teacher may at this point give out the correct notation of the bass line for students to sing.

Fifth Listening

Students focus on tempo, entering tempo markings, and any other comments regarding tempo on their forms. The "B" and "C" themes in this rondo are interesting but largely unsingable. The students might be asked to comment on them but not to deal with them in depth.

The completed listening chart for this composition will be more or less as given here:

Listening Chart

Work: Cello Concerto in D Major, Op. 101

Composer: Joseph Haydn   Dates: 1732–1820

Style: Viennese Classical

Form	Instruments	Dynamics	Tempo	Maj/min	Other
A	cello	mf	moderately fast	major	
A	tutti	f	allegretto		
B	cello				
A	cello				flutes
A	tutti				
C	cello				
A	cello				some variation in theme
A	orchestra			minor	
D	cello			major	low register
A	cello	mf to f throughout			
A	tutti				
Coda	cello/wwinds/ tutti	little variation in dynamics	little variation in tempo		wwinds alternate with with cello

---

MINUET AND TRIO FORM: INFORMATION
FOR THE TEACHER

A second form much used during this period was the minuet and trio, as the third movement of symphonies and other four-movement works by Mozart and Haydn and their contemporaries. Like the rondo, minuet and trio is an easy form to teach because it is short, and has much repetition. The basic minuet and trio is generally:

Minuet	Trio	Minuet
A	B	A
‖: a :‖‖: b :‖‖: a :‖	‖: c :‖‖: d :‖‖: c :‖	a b a

But sometimes is found as:

A	B	A
‖: a :‖‖: b :‖‖: c :‖	‖: c :‖‖: d :‖‖: c¹ :‖	a b a¹

In the latter instance the second a and c are variations and extensions of the first a and c. The minuet is a form based on a stately court dance in triple meter, popular during the eighteenth century. The trio is so called because in the earlier days it featured only three instruments; however this convention was no longer prevalent by the time Mozart and Haydn were composing their symphonies. There are often featured instruments in the trio section, but not necessarily three instruments.

Two minuet and trio movements recommended for study are the ones from Mozart's Symphony No. 41 in C Major, K. 551, the *Jupiter*, and from the same composer's serenade, Eine Kleine Nachtmusik, K. 525. The one from the *Jupiter* symphony will be dealt with in detail here. The notation and an abreviated teaching guide will be given for the first, since the basic teaching pattern would be the same for both.

LISTENING STRATEGY 3

Mozart, Symphony No. 41, K. 551: third movement, Minuet and Trio

Preparing for the First Listening Lesson

From the examples given thus far, it should be clear that students take a certain level of familiarity with a work even to a first listening. At the very least they have read and sung one of the principal themes or motives. In the previous examples a rhythm-erase exercise was used to present the rhythm, this being followed by the notation of the melody. This device is useful, but is not the only way to approach the first presentation of a theme. There are a number of options. The teacher may choose to:

- Sing the theme on a neutral syllable (*loo*) and then teach it by a rote process.
- Teach the theme through hand signs.
- Give the class the theme, notated in stem and solfa, to be read.

Sometimes these approaches may be combined. For example, if the class reads music with great difficulty, the teacher might first isolate the rhythm and meter through a rhythm erase exercise, then, when rhythmic problems have been solved, add the melody to the rhythm, singing on *loo*. When the melody begins to be familiar to the class, *solfa* and hand signs could be utilized to aid with the rote teaching, and, finally, the staff notation could be distributed and sung by sight.

When any of these approaches is used it must be followed by giving the staff notation to the students to be sung in *solfa*, and by having the students memorize the theme before the first listening. For this Mozart minuet and trio, let us look at the notation before deciding how to proceed.

MINUET

What problems immediately present themselves with this notation? What must the students know before this is given to them?

Rhythm

They must be facile with $\frac{3}{4}$ meter, and if they have not encountered eighth rests previously, these will have to be introduced.

Procedure: Have the students read:

Then have them inner hear every other eighth note. Show the notation for what they have performed as:

Because of the alternation of the ♩ ♩ ♩ pattern with the ♪ ♪ ♪ pattern in this theme, students might benefit from reading the rhythm in *ta*'s, *ti*'s and *too*'s before reading the *solfa*. A rhythm-erase procedure is probably warranted.

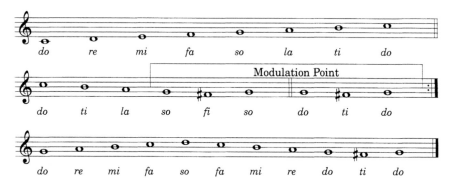

Melody

The minuet theme modulates in the third phrase from C-*do* to G-*do*. To prepare students for this, sing with them, using *solfa* and hand signs:

do   re   mi   fa   so   la   ti   do

Modulation Point

do   ti   la   so   fi   so   do   ti   do

do   re   mi   fa   so   fa   mi   re   do   ti   do

Make a clear aural comparison of d^l - t - d^l with s - fi - s. To make the modulation visually clear as well, staff notation should be given to the students rather than stem and *solfa*. Staff notation will also make the identification of the sequence (phrase 2) more obvious.

First Listening

Students must be told that the entire four phrases they can sing now consitute an "A" section of the minuet and are asked to chart the form. Mozart used the second, more complex form for this minuet and trio. Because of the extensions and variations of the "A" theme and the "C" theme, it is recommended that only the first minuet section, "A," be used for this first listening.

Students should listen and make notes on their listening charts, discuss their findings, and then listen again to make corrections. They can be instructed to use

"V" for variation to show that the section is an "A"—it is similar—but that there are differences.

The minuet form should eventually be shown as:

minuet: a, a, b, a, b, a$_v$

Second Listening

The music for the opening of the trio section should now be sung and memorized by the students.

TRIO

The students may then hear the entire movement and complete their form diagramming.

Third Listening

Instrumentation: *What instruments are playing the theme at each entrance? Is there any marked charge in the instrumentation within sections? What instruments have solos in the trio section?*

Fourth Listening

Dynamic Structure: The dynamics are very regular throughout the minuet section: piano for the first two phrases of the theme, forte for the last two. The trio section begins softly, then has a sudden forte followed by piano. Students should listen to discover this dynamic structure, and mark their listening charts accordingly.

Fifth Listening

Harmonization: Students should sing *do* (I) *and so* (V) with the minuet theme to derive the probable harmony. They could then sing Mozart's bass line with the melody:

Question: *Since the bass part is a single note line, where is the rest of the harmony? Where are the I and V chords?* They do not occur as chords, but as broken chords above the bass, played by the second violins:

This kind of bass is very frequent in works by Haydn and Mozart, and has a special name, *Alberti bass*, after an earlier composer who used this technique extensively. Students should try singing the *Alberti bass* with the bass line and with the melody (first violin part). When they listen this time it should be to follow the bass line and the *Alberti bass*. They may also be asked to mark where they hear a change to the minor (the "D" section in the trio).

No column has been given to tempo because it is absolutely regular. Mozart's marking is allegretto. This information is shown after the form is named. Student attention should be drawn to the fact that, thus far, there has been no great tempo variation. Later, comparisons may be drawn with works of other periods and styles in which there is considerable variation in tempo. Regular tempo is a characteristic of the Viennese classical style.

Listening Chart

Work: Symphony No. 41 in C Major, The *Jupiter*, K. 551

Composer: Wolfgang Amadeus Mozart   Dates: 1756–91

Style: Viennese Classical   Form: Minuet and Trio (Allegretto)

Overall Form	Form within Sections	Instrumentation	Dynamics	Other
A	a	Strings	*p f*	
	a		*p f*	
	b		*p f*	
	a(v)		*p f*	theme in canon
	b		*p f*	
	a(v)		*p f*	theme in canon
B	c	flute & oboe		
	c			
	d		*ff p*	minor
	c(v)			
	d		*ff p*	minor
	c(v)			
A	a	Strings	*p f*	
	b		*p f*	

LISTENING STRATEGY

Mozart, *Eine Kleine Nachtmusik*, K. 525, third movement, *Allegretto*

The second minuet and trio movement suggested for teaching is also by Mozart, the third movement (Allegretto) of his serenade, *Eine Kleine Nachtmusik*, K. 525. In this lighter work for string orchestra the minuet and trio form is clearly presented. For younger students this might be considered as the first listening example in this form.

MINUET THEME

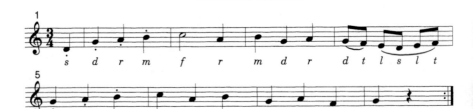

TRIO THEME

For singing, both of these themes have been notated an octave below their score notation, although they appear in the correct keys. Students' attention should be drawn to the fact that they sing these themes an octave lower than the strings play them.

The minuet theme is easily singable. Attention should be paid to the staccato and legato markings and these two terms may be taught. In measures six and seven there are trills not shown in the notation for singing. Students will hear these and no doubt comment on them. The subject of ornamentation in music could be discussed at this point, and students could experiment with adding trills at the cadences of known songs.

Some discussion should follow as to whether ornamentation really suits folk songs. This is not a yes or no question. Many composers have used ornamentation in their settings of folk music. The students may recall Mozart's setting of "Twinkle, Twinkle Little Star" as a case in point.

The trio section holds some problems. It is highly chromatic. If students appear ready, the ascending chromatic scale could be introduced:

do di re ri me fa fi so si la li ti do[3]

If students are still struggling with diatonic music it is not advisable to introduce chromaticism. In this case, the rhythm of the trio can be shown in notation and the melody either taught by rote or simply heard. The harmonies in both the minuet and the trio are basically I - V with cadences on I - IV - V - I.

---

[3] A superscript is used to designate notes above the seventh degree of the scale, and a subscript is used to designate notes below the first degree of the scale.

Chapter 5

The Symphony
and Sonata Forms

Information for the Teacher

Haydn, referred to for many years as the father of the symphony, was a prolific composer in this form, if not the actual inventor of it. His 104 symphonies established the basic conventions of symphonic composition followed by every composer since. Mozart and Beethoven knew and respected his work.

The symphonic form that evolved with Haydn was a four-movement work with a first movement in sonata form, a slow second movement, a third movement in a $\frac{3}{4}$ dance pattern and a fast final movement usually in either sonata or rondo form.

We have already examined a rondo movement and a minuet and trio. It is now important to begin a study of the sonata form so integral to symphonic writing.

SONATA FORM

No study of the music of Haydn and Mozart can ignore this most significant musical form, which was given its definition by Haydn and Mozart, and was used extensively by them and by composers since, well into the twentieth-century.

In choosing a work through which to introduce this complex form, the teacher should attempt to find an example in which the development section is not too long and in which the treatment of the motives or themes is straightforward and easy to follow. The basic outline of sonata form is:

1. An exposition section
   A theme is introduced and stated in the home key of the work—referred to as the tonic key. After a bridge passage a new theme of a contrasting nature is introduced in another key, often in the related minor or major to the first theme, or in the dominant key.

2. A development section

   Themes or parts of themes (motives) heard in the exposition are now varied, expanded, stated in other keys, and, in general, experimented with musically. Changes may be made to the themes or motives in pitch level, rhythm, tempo, and dynamics. Mode may shift from major to minor. Accompanying parts may be altered. Voices may enter in canon or new countermelodies may appear against the themes. This is followed by a section that leads back to the original (tonic) key. (Bridge; Transition)

3. A recapitulation section

   The themes are restated as they were in the first section, the exposition, except that all are now given in the tonic key.

4. A coda

   Brings the movement to a close.

LISTENING STRATEGY 5

Haydn, Symphony No. 104 in D Major, First Movement

INTRODUCTION

This dramatic opening, just two bars long, presents two problems for students. The first, and most important, is its tonality. Listen to these opening bars without seeing the notation. Is this section major or minor? It is impossible to tell until we hear the next notes. As preparation for listening to this, one activity should be the singing of numerous songs in diatonic major, natural minor, and harmonic minor, classifying them according to scale and singing these scales in *solfa* and with handsigns.

DIATONIC MAJOR (LAUGHING SINGING)

NATURAL MINOR CANON

HARMONIC MINOR (AH POOR BIRD)

Ah,   poor   bird   take   your   flight,

far   a - bove   the   sor - rows   of   this   sad   night.

First Listening

Play just the first two bars. *Is this in major or in minor?* Discussion should follow. There will probably be disagreement among the students. To resolve this, divide
the class into two sections:

1. Using hand-signs, have group one softly sing a sustained *do* while group two
   sings a sustained *so*. The teacher then adds (sings) a clear *mi* for the class to hear.
2. Without changing actual pitch, the group singing *do* is led by hand signs to
   sing *la* and the group singing *so* changes the *solfa* syllable to *mi*. The teacher
   adds the *do*.

Which voice tells us whether we are in major or minor? (The third; the *mi* in major,
the *do* in minor). The quality of a chord (major or minor) is determined by the third
degree of the scale. Teaching note: To lead to a change in tonality without a change
in pitch, show the *solfa* hand-sign being sung with one hand, then show the new *solfa*
sign beside it:

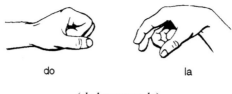

do   la

(*do* becomes *la*)

At this point the class should return to the recording. *Let's listen to a bit more to hear whether Haydn used major or minor in his introduction to this symphony.* (Minor.)

The second problem in the introduction is the rhythm. The double dotted note will require some explanation. Students should be reminded that the dotted quarter note represents a quarter tied to an eighth note:

and that, by extension of this principle, a dotted eighth is equal to an eighth tied to a sixteenth note:

If students understand this much they will be able to extrapolate the idea that a dot is worth half the value of the note it follows. *What note is the second dot following? It is actually following a dot, but what note is that dot replacing?* (A sixteenth note.) *What would be half as long as a sixteenth note?* (A thirty-second note.) *This is the value of the second dot:*

The note following must be a very short one. It is the other half of the thirty-second note pair:

It occupies the same overall duration as ♪♪, but the first sound is longer and the second is very short.

Second Listening

With these two technical problems out of the way, the class may now focus on the music of the opening section. Questions:

1. *What is the overall character of this opening?* (Avoid simplistic, happy-sad responses. The purpose of this question is to elicit good descriptive words that can be used in a comparative way with the second theme when it is introduced.)
2. *What instruments are prominent?*
3. *How many times did Haydn use that important-sounding eighth-note introduction?*

The listening chart should be filled in to show this information.

Third Listening

After reviewing students' comments about the character of the first theme, the tape or disc may be played again, this time continuing to the end of the exposition section. *What is the character of the second theme?* (Sharply contrasted to the first; major mode; fast tempo; bright, lively.)

The music for the second theme should then be distributed, sung, analyzed and discussed. Tonic, dominant harmonies could be added to it.

NOTATION

Information to Be Given to the Students

*In the section of this movement we have been listening to, Haydn has present-
ed us with two important themes, the first in minor and the second in the related major. This first section, where the themes are introduced to the listener, is
called the exposition.*

*Now, Haydn goes on to work with parts of these themes. In particular he takes
a small part of the second theme, measures three and four as a motive, and
works and reworks them in this next section, the development.*

*What could we do with this small motive so that we could repeat it many times
but still make it interesting? How could we vary it?* Students may make suggestions about tempo, dynamics, pitch level, and harmonization. Their suggestions could be placed on the chalkboard. If suggestions are not immediately
forthcoming suggest that they refer back to charts they have kept from previous listenings.

What are some of the ways composers varied other themes we have heard?
With a list of possibilities on the board students listen to the recording to determine which of their suggestions were actually used by Haydn: changes in
pitch, use of sequences, changes in mode and harmonization and variations in
dynamic level and timbre.

Fourth Listening

The focus of this lesson is the closing section of the first movement, the recapitulation. Student should be asked to identify where this begins by raising hands. It
is a complete restatement of the second theme in its original key, D Major. Even now,
Haydn gives us variation, following the exact restatement in the strings with a ren-
dering by one flute and two oboes.

The coda is a brilliant brass fanfare, recalling the motive used in the development section.

Summary

Clearly, there are many layers to be uncovered in this work. It could be listened
to many more times both for further learning and for enjoyment. But as an initial example of sonata form it will have served its purpose at this point.

The listening chart completed by students should be somewhat different for this
work. It must allow for more leeway in responses.

Listening Chart

Work: Symphony No. 104 in D major

Composer: Franz Joseph Haydn   Dates: 1732–1809

Style: Viennese Classical   Form: Sonata Allegro

		Character	Mode	Instrumentation	Dynamics	Tempo
1. Exposition	Introduction	strong, stately, serious	minor, shifting to major and then back	brasses & ww followed by strings	f followed by p; alternating	Adagio (slow)
	Main Theme	lively, cheerful, energetic	Major	strings	mf with use of < and >	Andante (fast)
2. Development		6-note motive; changes in pitch level, use of sequences, major-minor shifts, use of different instruments to create changes in timbre, changes in dynamic level, in harmonization.				
3. Recapitulation		First Statement as it was in the Exposition, followed by a quiet statement by 2 oboes and a flute. This is followed by 2 measures of silence before the final play with the 6-note motive leading to the coda.				
4. Coda		A brass fanfare based on the 6 note motive.				

THE MUSIC OF LUDWIG VAN BEETHOVEN

Information for the Teacher

The music of Beethoven is difficult to pigeonhole as classical or romantic. While clearly strongly influenced by the music of Mozart and Haydn, Beethoven's music, from the time of the writing of his Third Symphony, the *Eroica*, foreshadowed such romantic composers as Berlioz, Liszt, and Brahms. He used classical forms; however he expanded and enlarged these forms greatly. His symphonies are much longer than those of Mozart and Haydn.

Further, within these expanded classical forms he exhibited a tension and excitement far removed from the restraint of classicism. His reputed stormy temperament is evident in his music, which is both dramatic and powerful.

Technically, his music marked a departure from classicism as well. He enlarged the symphony orchestra, both in numbers and in kinds of instruments, adding trombones, piccolo, and contrabassoon and he used instruments such as the double bass and timpani in an unusual manner, sometimes giving them thematic material rather than the simple accompaniments they had enjoyed in the past. He marked tempo, dynamics, and expressive indicators into his scores with abandon. When he found traditional Italian terminology inhibiting, he did not hesitate to write in plain words in his own language what he wanted:

This piece is to be played with great feeling.[1]

The music of Beethoven with its great contrasts in mood, its intensity, its grandeur, clearly marked a turning point in the history of music.

Two works will be presented here for study, The Sixth Symphony (the *Pastoral*) and the Fifth Piano Concerto (the *Emperor*). Other works not dealt with here, but highly recommended for study are the Third Symphony (the *Eroica*), the Ninth Symphony, and Beethoven's only opera, *Fidelio*.

LISTENING STRATEGY 6

Beethoven, Symphony No. 6 in F Major, Op. 68, *Pastoral:* Mvts 3, 4, and 5

No man can love the country as much as I do. Woods, trees, and rocks supply that echo that man desires.[2]

While Beethoven cautioned his audiences that this work is *more an expression of feeling than tone painting*, his descriptive titles for each section, and the music itself, with its cuckoo calls, shepherd's pipe tunes, country dance, and thunderstorm clearly point the way to programmatic works of later composers. Beethoven entitled the sections of this symphony:

- Awakening of Joyful Feelings on Arriving in the Country
- Joyful Gathering of the Country Folk
- Storm

---

[1] Quartet in E Minor, Op. 59, No. 2

[2] Martin Hürliman, ed. *Beethoven: Briefe und Gespräche*, Zurich, 1944, p.54. As quoted by Bernstein and Picher in *An Introduction to Music*, 3rd Edition, Prentice Hall, 1966.

- Shepherd's Song
- Grateful and Glad Feelings After the Storm

In the following guided listening experiences we will be using only the last four of these, which comprise the third, fourth, and fifth movements. It is unusual for a symphony to have five movements, and even less usual for these movements to flow one into the next without descernable closure between movements. This symphony represents a major departure from the patterns established by Haydn and Mozart.

It is suggested that before introducing this work to students the teacher listen to it several times to become familiar with the themes and to fit Beethoven's descriptive titles to the music.

The focus of this series of listening lessons will not be on form, as it was with the previous compositions, but on those aspects of this work that make it a departure from previous compositional practices: Beethoven's use of dynamics, the expanded orchestra, and the highly descriptive nature of the music.

Preparation

Dynamics   What do students need to know before listening? Since one of the characteristics of Beethoven is his use of a much broader spectrum of dynamic levels than his predecessors, this is probably the time to introduce the full range of dynamic possibilities, with correct terminology, to the students:

softer	pianissimo	*pp*
	piano	*p*
	mezzo piano	*mp*
	mezzo forte	*mf*
	forte	*f*
louder	fortissimo	*ff*

Scores show Beethoven's dynamic markings with up to four forte markings: *ffff*. The crescendo and decrescendo are widely used by Beethoven, as is the technique of suddenly becoming soft or loud: subito piano, subito forte. Students should be led to experiment with these various dynamic levels and techniques, applying them to their own compositions as well as to their song repertory.

They should keep a page in their notebooks with this traditional dynamic terminology so that they will be able to refer to it when making decisions about their own performances or when trying to determine what is happening in music to which they are listening.

Instruments   Beethoven was the first composer to use the trombone in the symphony. He also added the contrabassoon and the piccolo. These instruments, perhaps already familiar to students, should be reviewed and added under the correct families in students' notebooks.

Harmony   The harmonic structure used by Beethoven is, like that of Mozart and Haydn, strongly tonic-dominant. However, there is an increase in the use of secondary chords. The triads drill and the chord progressions studied earlier should be reviewed so that the new ones discovered in this music may be added to them.

The Music   Since three movements to be studied create a scenario—the country folk gather, they dance, their festivities are interrupted by a thunderstorm, and as the storm moves away the shepherd horns are heard and the people express *glad and grateful feelings*—they should be presented in that order.

   The first themes to be taught are the two representing the "Joyful Gathering of the Country Folk" and the one that is the peasant dance. Beethoven did not specifically identify the latter but it is clearly such, and Berlioz later referred to this section as picturing "Mountaineers in their Heavy Sabots." Gone are the dignified minuets of the Mozart and Haydn symphonies. In their place is a vigorous duple meter romp. The form is basically A B A C A in this third movement.

JOYFUL GATHERING THEME

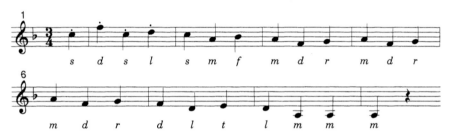

JOYFUL GATHERING, THEME NO. 2

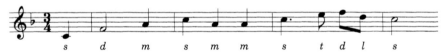

First Listening

   After reading and memorizing the first two principal themes of this movement, the students may be given the Listening Chart (page 120) with the section under "form" filled in.

   At the first hearing they should be asked to determine what instruments are playing the A, B, and C themes, and whether they can pick out any of the accompanying voices (bassoon; double basses). They should discuss their answers in class and listen again to make any needed corrections in their charting.

Second Listening

   This experience is to focus on Beethoven's use of dynamics in this movement. Students should keep notes on the chart while listening and then compare their responses. The teacher may then show them the actual markings used by Beethoven

Listening Chart

Work: Symphony No. 6 in F Major, Op. 68 *Pastoral*, 3rd Movement (Allegro)

Composer: Ludwig van Beethoven

Style: Viennese Classical

Form	Instruments	Dynamics	Other
a	strings, detached then legato	*p, mf, f*	shifts in key; theme modulates
	brass bridge to b		at each entrance
b	flute with bassoon; clarinet	*p to pp*	bassoon accompanyment on
	followed by French horn	*mp to mf*	d(1) s d muted horn sound
a	upper strings; double bass	*crescendo to f*	
	lead into C		
c	strings on theme; double bass	*ff*	strongly rhythmic "peasant
	accompanyment on d d f d		dance" scale: d r m f s l ta d
a	strings; detatched then legato	*p*	
	horns leading into next	*crescendo to ff*	character of the music changes
	movement		abruptly as the "storm"
			approaches

and a further listening could be done to determine whether the orchestra and conductor in the recording followed Beethoven's suggested dynamics accurately.

Third Listening

Modulation: The A theme is interesting in that its two parts are sharply contrasted; the first section moves quickly and is detached while the second is legato. Further, the second ends on low *so*, which becomes *do* in the next statement of the first part of the theme, thus causing repeated key shifts.

To hear this, students will need to sing the A theme, changing the last *so* to *do* and beginning again in the new key. After trying this they should listen to identify the key shifts in the A section.

Fourth Listening

Mixolydian Mode: Sing a selection of folk songs in the mixolydian mode. Three beautiful examples in this mode are the English ballad "Poor Sally Sits A-Weeping," the Australian "Last Farewell to Stirling," and the Appalachian song "The Good Old Man."[3] The character of mixolydian is major, but it has a flattened seventh degree:

---
[3] Found in the *Kodály Method*, Revised Edition, Lois Choksy. Prentice Hall, 1988 pp. 236–37.

THE GOOD OLD MAN

Where   are   you   go - ing   my   good   old   man

Where   are   you   go - ing   my   hon- ey   my   lamb

Best   old   soul   in   the   world.

PEASANT DANCE (THEME, COMPLETE)

d   r   d   s   l   t   d   r   d   s

f   s   l   ta   d   d   r   s   s   d   f

Students should derive the scales of their mixolydian songs to discover the need for a flat on the seventh degree, changing *ti* to *ta*. The handsign for the flattened *ti* may be taught:

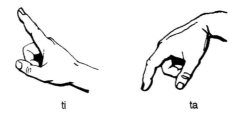

ti   ta

Handsign for *ti* to *ta*

They should then sing the C theme, the "Peasant Dance." Two factors give this section a mixolydian character. The flattened seventh and the *do, fa, do* accompaniment in the bass:

d   d   f   d   f   d   d   f   d   f   d

When the C theme has been analyzed and memorized, the whole third movement should be heard once again and the chart completed with any additional comments students wish to make, under "other."

Fifth Listening

It is probably a good idea to leave this work for a period before continuing to the next movement. When it is approached, the third movement should be played in its entirety. This can be a nondirected listening. Students by this time know this part of the work well enough to listen attentively.

When the end of the third movement is reached, the teacher should simply allow the tape or disc to continue.

What do you think is happening? What is Beethoven picturing in the music? How does he achieve that effect?

The "Storm" section of the symphony, the fourth movement, really requires no more involved teaching.

The Fifth Movement

This last movement is introduced by a call that brings to mind shepherd's pipes:

INTRODUCTION TO FIFTH MOVEMENT

The horn's answer to the clarinet is on the fifth degree of the scale. Both instruments are strongly in the tonic until the last two measures, when there is a shift from C major to the key of F in preparation for the principal theme of this movement.

A THEME

It is important that students know the A theme very well, since it is sometimes hidden in this movement. What follows is loosely in rondo form: A B A C A D A, Coda.

B THEME

C THEME

Preparation

Students will need to be familiar with the V_7 chord to work with the harmonization of this theme. Sing songs in which this chord is outlined:

CHERUBINI CANON NO. 1

Pull the V_7 out of the melody. Sing the pitches as they occur in the tune: *fa, re, ti, so* and then simultaneously, to hear the sound of a seventh added to the 1 - 3 - 5 of the triad. Students may well ask if this can be done to other chords. The answer, of course, is yes.

FIE, NAY PRITHEE, JOHN

Henry Purcell (1659–95)

How many 7 chords can you identify in the last phrase of this song? (Five). Sing each as it occurs in the song:

vii⁷   la, fa, re, ti

vi⁷   so, mi, do, la

v⁷   fa, re, ti, so

IV⁷   mi, do, la, fa

iii⁷   re, ti, so, mi

and then as simultaneous chords. Return to the triads drill and add a 7th degree to each triad.

Procedure   Give the students the first phrase of the A theme in either stem and *solfa* or in staff notation. Read the phrase together, correcting any problems. Memorize it.

Is this a question phrase or an answer phrase? (Question.) *Create an answer phrase to go with it. Use the rhythm of the first phrase, the notes of the I chord and V₇ chord in constructing your answer phrase.*

This activity may be done orally (improvisation) or in writing (composition). The oral has the advantage that responses do not become fixed in the mind as they may once written down. We want students to remember the Beethoven answer phrase.

First Listening

After hearing students' answer phrases, play the recording as far as the end of the third statement. Sing Beethoven's answer phrase. This may be done in *solfa*, or a neutral syllable (loo) if *solfa* is more of a hindrance than an aid. It may be necessary to listen again to be sure the response is correct.

Students should then notate the second phrase under the first phrase as it was notated and distributed by the teacher.

Second Listening

The A Theme:

List the instruments playing the A theme in these first three statements. Note the dynamics on your chart, also.

Third Listening

This time we are going to listen to the entire 5th movement of this symphony. Each time you hear the A theme return, list it as "A" under "Form" on your charts. When you hear other themes, call them B, C, and so forth as we have done in the past. What comes before the first A statement? (A short introduction played by the clarinet and answered in a lower place by the French horn.) Students should sing this introduction before listening.

It is unlikely that many students will aurally perceive the return to A after the C theme. If some do, this creates good discussion and the necessity to listen again to find the answer. In this statement the actual melody as introduced at the beginning of the work is absent.

In its place the strings play around the melody in scale patterns. However the implication of the melody is strong. In the repeated listening students should be encouraged to sing the A theme with this section. Once they have done so they will not fail to hear it the next time.

Fourth Listening

Sing the A Theme. Harmonize it using do (I), fa (IV) and so (V). Listen to hear whether Beethoven's harmonization is the same as yours. (It isn't.) Here is the bass line used by Beethoven. Sing this with the theme:

HARMONIZATION OF A THEME

Fifth Listening

Sing the B and C themes. List the dynamics used in these theme statements and any other information that will help you identify them.

Sixth Listening

What kind of form does this appear to be in? (rondo - A B A C A D A). *What generally happens at the end of a rondo?* (A coda.) *Where did Beethoven take the ending of his coda theme from?* (The introduction.)

Follow-Up Activities

Students should be encouraged to read and discuss Beethoven's life. His inability in later life to hear his own music, except in his head, his deafness, which was already advanced when he composed this symphony, astounds students. In a popular idiom, the Disney treatment of the symphony in *Fantasia* might appeal to some students.

Listening Chart			
Work: Symphony No. 6 in F Major, (*Pastoral*), Fifth Movement			
Composer: Ludwig van Beethoven			**Dates: 1770–1827**
Style: Transitional (Viennese Classical—Romantic)			

Form	Instruments	Dynamics	Other
Introduction	flute and horn		
	a ⁞ violins	*p*	accompaniment
A	a ⁞ violas/cellos	<	in bass
	a ⁞ winds	*f*	
B	flute leads back to A	*f*	key change
		< >	key change back to F
	a ⁞ violins	*p*	
A	a ⁞ violas		
	a ⁞ horns lead to C	*p* < *f*	key change at end
C	winds punctuated by strings	*mf* *p*	
		alternating	key change
	a ⁞ violins on scale passages around		A theme is hidden
	theme notes	*mp*	in scale passages.
A	a ⁞ violas on scales	*mp* < *f*	Bass as in first
	a ⁞ cellos on scales	*f*	theme
B	cellos, violins alternating	*f*	return to F at end
	a ⁞ cellos alone	much variation in	
A	a ⁞ violins and violas	dynamic levels	fragments of A
	a ⁞ cellos on scales	*p* at end	theme
Coda	violin scale passages on notes	*p* at end	hymn-like closing
	of introduction	*p* *f* alternating	
		ff at end	

LISTENING STRATEGY 7

Beethoven, Piano Concerto No. 5 in E♭ Major, Op. 73: Second Movement

The second Beethoven composition suggested for study is the second movement of his Piano Concerto No. 5 in E♭ Major, the *Emperor*. This work is chosen not only because of its singable melody, but also because its tempo, *Adagio un poco mosso*, is not one encountered in the works previously studied. Only the principal theme will be dealt with. This is a short movement, but rich in beauty.

The orchestra opens this movement with a slow, soft, complete statement of the theme. After this the piano enters on high F, plays what is essentially a descending scale motive, before leading into a beautifully simple rendition of the theme, supported by a broken triad bass and pizzicato strings. In the next statement of the theme, the woodwinds have the melody and the piano plays the broken chord accompaniment in an upper register in counterpoint to it. At the end of this short movement, in the key of B major, the orchestra makes a sharp, almost shocking harmonic change, *do* to *ti*, and the piano plays a new melody (*ti* becomes *so*) in the key of E♭ major, which leads suddenly into the wild romp that is the last movement, rondo.

Preparation

The reading and memorization of this theme will be helped by some prior analysis. Students should have the notation of the theme, with measures numbered:

BEETHOVEN CONCERTO

Melody

How did Beethoven use repetition? Are any two measures the same?
(5 & 6, 13 & 14)

Are any two parts of phrases similar?
(10 same as 11, 12, 3, except for an expansion of the rhythm)

Is there any use of sequence or sequence-like patterns?
(7, 8, 9 - consecutive ascending patterns).

Where does the melody first sound as if it might be the end, the final cadence on do? (10)

First Listening

Harmonization: *Does the melody come to a stopping point, I, the tonic, at measure 10 as we thought it would?* (No.) *Let's follow the bass part as we listen.* Notation should be distributed.

In measure 10, where we thought there would be a cadence to do *(I), what note did Beethoven give us?* (la, vi). *Let's sing the two cadences:* I V I (authentic) and I V vi (deceptive).

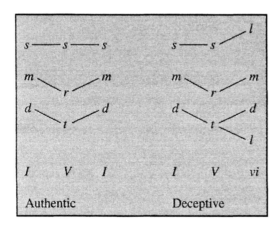

The deceptive cadence was used extensively by Mozart and Beethoven. It's like a prolonged good-bye, a lingering in the doorway. Students should try singing the bass line softly with the recording.

Second Listening

Articulation, pizzicato and legato, first theme statement: *Strings may be played in two ways. They may be plucked (pizzicato) or bowed (legato). Both are used in this movement. Where do the basses change from pizzicato to legato?* (Measure 6, last note.)

Third Listening

How many times does Beethoven present us with this theme? (Three) How does he make it different each time?

First entrance   orchestra, chords
Second entrance   piano with Alberti bass
Third entrance   woodwinds on melody, piano on Alberti bass.

Fourth Listening

The overall character of this movement is soft, piano, but there is an interesting use of crescendo and decrescendo. Where do these happen in the first statement?

7, 8, 9   *crescendo to* f
10   *decrescendo to* p
11   f *decrescendo to* p

Fifth Listening

Entire movement: This should be a nondirected listening, purely for enjoyment. Students could make notes on their listening charts if they wish, but should not feel compelled to do so. At the end of the movement the teacher might allow the tape or disc to continue for a few moments so that the students have a taste of the last movement.

Listening Chart
Work: Piano Concerto No. 5 in E♭ Major, Op. 73, The *Emperor*
Composer: Ludwig van Beethoven   **Dates: 1770–1827**
Style: Transitional (Viennese Classical—Romantic)

Theme	Accompaniment	Dynamics	Other
orchestra	string basses pizzicato then legato	piano with $<\;>$	deceptive cadence m. 10
piano entrance	broken chord-piano chords-orchestra	*p*	change of key
piano	orchestra	louder	
orchestra	piano on broken chords	piano with $<\;>$	ending with do-ti, ti becomes so in new key of E♭

CONCLUSION

The material in this chapter has comprised a year's work if music is taught twice or three times weekly. It has focused extensively on art music of one style and period, the Viennese classical, but in the course of this study may other aspects of music have been presented. All elements of music have been brought to students' attention: melody, harmony, rhythm, tempo, timbre, dynamics, and form. All the activities through which music can be learned have been utilized: singing, playing, moving, listening, reading, writing, and creating.

Three specific forms have been introduced: rondo, sonata allegro, and minuet and trio. All triads have been introduced in root position as has the need for inversion to create comfortable voice leading. Cadences I-V; I-IV and V-vi have been analyzed and sung and the intervals of major and minor seconds and thirds were introduced. Five scales have been studied: the major, three forms of minor, and mixolydian.

Through all the above the focus has been where it must be, on music… on great music that is worthy of study.

This and all the music studied during the year should be available at listening stations in the music room or library so that students may return to it as they wish. Lists of easily obtainable recordings of the works studied should also be given to students.

Chapter 6

Experiences in Directed Listening: Music of the Baroque (1600–1750)

BACKGROUND INFORMATION FOR THE TEACHER

The Baroque was a period of tremendous musical outpouring throughout Europe. It saw in Italy such masters as Monteverdi (1567–1643), Frescobaldi (1583–1643), Corelli (1653–1713), Scarlatti (1660–1725) and Vivaldi (1678–1741). In Germany this period produced Schütz (1585–1672), Buxtehude (1637–1707), Telemann (1681–1767), and J. S. Bach (1685–1750); while in France it saw Lully (1632–87), Couperin (1668–1733) and Rameau (1683–1764). It was the period in England of Purcell (1659–95) and Handel (1685–1759).

In the visual arts, Rembrandt, Rubens, Velasquez, and Bernini created masterpieces, while in the sciences this period produced Newton (1642–1727) and Galileo (1564–1642). There can be little doubt that it was one of the most creative periods in the history of humanity. It saw the development in vocal music of the oratorio, the opera, the cantata, the aria, and the recitative, while in instrumental music it produced or further developed the fugue, concerto, sonata, suite, chorale prelude, passacaglia, chaconne, toccata, and rondeau.

During the Baroque period there were essentially only three ways for a composer to make a living. He could write music for the entertainment of the court of one of the many princes, electors, or other minor or major nobility; he could work as a church musician, playing the organ, directing the choirs, and composing for the services, or he could teach. Many did all three. The music of the period clearly reflects this. It consisted almost entirely of instrumental music and operas produced for the upper classes, organ and choral works for the church, and studies for students. The only place the common man customarily heard serious music was in church.

The two undisputed musical giants of the period were Johann Sebastian Bach (1685–1750), who spent all but one short period of his life as a church musician and teacher, and George Frideric Handel (1685–1759) who spent many years of his life writing music for the entertainment of the court of the British monarchy.

The musical examples for teaching presented in this chapter are drawn from the works of these two composers.

132

Characteristics of Baroque Music

Music of this period has great unity. In one piece, one mood prevails throughout. If a rhythm pattern is stated at the beginning it is heard again and again until the end of the movement or piece. This tends to give a feeling of unity and of forward motion to pieces. Melodies are similarly repeated many times.

In dynamics, scores were not generally marked p and f. Once a dynamic level is set, it remains at that level throughout the section or even throughout the entire work. The exception to this rule is "terraced dynamics," in which two contrasting dynamic levels are alternated. When the dynamic level shifts, the change is always sudden. There are no crescendos and decrescendos; no gradual building or diminishing.

The Baroque saw the rise of "monophony," the accompanied solo song in opera, oratorio, and cantata, and the further development of "polyphony." Polyphony may be described loosely as two or three (or more) melodies, equally important, all happening at the same time. "Counterpoint" is the compositional technique through which a polyphonic texture is produced. The sounding together of the melodies creates chords and harmonies, but the music is conceived and perceived horizontally rather than vertically.

Instruments of the Period

One of the most important instruments of the Baroque was the pipe organ. It was this that lead to the great fugues and chorale preludes of Bach.

Baroque Organ

Basically the Baroque organ is a set of tuned pipes fed by air from a bellows, and controlled from a keyboard. In a large organ there are several sets of pipes, each with its own particular tone color and dynamic level. These have alternate air-feeding channels, controlled by "stops" on the organ. There can be as many as eighty of these on a Baroque organ. Among these are "reed" stops with soft, flutelike sounds, string stops, solo stops, and stops for combining sounds.

Pipes are divided into sections identified as:

- great
- choir
- positive
- pedal

The last of these, pedal, is the lowest and loudest and is played with the feet on a large keyboard below the instrument.

Baroque organs are highly decorated. They are often works of art in themselves. Many reproductions of Baroque style organs have been built for North American churches. If at all possible, students should be taken to see and hear one of these. Barring this possibility, pictures, slides, and videos are a viable alternative.

The other instruments that became very important during this period are strings. In Italy, in Cremona, the Amati family—father, sons and grandsons—were producing violins unlike any that had been heard before; and their student Antonio Stradivarius brought violin making to an art never reached before or since. It was during this period that strings became the core of the orchestra, a position maintained to this day.

Harpsichord and clavichord were also important instruments, the former as a part of the Baroque orchestra, the latter, with its smaller tone, used in more intimate settings. The equal-distance tuning of the keyboard into twelve mathematically precise semitones (where it had previously been tuned via the overtone system) made possible for the first time compositions and performances in every key.

Other instruments used commonly in the Baroque orchestra were recorders, flutes, oboes, trumpets (valveless), horns, and timpani. However, the standardized orchestra "families" of the classical period did not yet exist. Composers exercised flexibility in instrumentation.

Forms contained little contrast. Often a single musical idea is heard throughout a work. There are no sharply contrasting themes within movements, as with Mozart and Haydn. There is contrast from movement to movement within longer works, but not within the movements.

Harmony tends to change in a very regular way. This can be every measure, or at some other set distance.

One of the most interesting devices of the period is the use of the "basso-continuo" or figured bass. The bass part was written out in full but only numbers specified the chords to be played above it. At the harpsichord, the performer played the notated "continuo" part with the left hand and improvised the right within the framework of the chords indicated by the numbers. (This is in some ways similar to performances today from jazz "charts.")

To choose just three or four compositions from this 150 years of massive creativity is daunting. However, the purpose is to introduce students to a few characteristic works in such a way that they will be inclined, or perhaps even compelled, to explore further. To this end the following listening strategies will introduce students to a fugue, a concerto grosso, and a suite.

LISTENING STRATEGY No. 8

J.S. Bach: The Fugue from The *Toccata* and Fugue in D minor for Organ.

Information for the Teacher

A fugue is a polyphonic composition in which a theme, called the "subject," is first stated in one voice and then imitated by other voices throughout the entire piece. The subject generally alternates between statements in the home key, the "tonic," and statements in the "dominant" (V) of that key.

The first section ends when each voice has stated the subject once. This section is referred to as the "Exposition."

In the middle there can be modulation to other keys or shifts from major to minor or minor to major. Connecting these are "Episodes," short sections without the theme.

At the end the theme returns to the home key and a coda closes the work.

What do students need to know to listen with understanding?

- canons and canonic entrances at the 5th and 8th.
- augmentation and diminution.
- sequences.
- changes in mode: major-minor
- i-V harmonization in minor.

Canons and Canonic Entrances at the 5th and 8th.

Most students have sung rounds; "Brother John," "Three Blind Mice," "Scotland's Burning." Rounds are a type of canon in which one voice enters and follows after the other at the same beginning pitch. The term "canon" includes all such imitative singing, even when the voices enter at different pitches. The following canon is like a round in that each voice imitates the one before, but it is unlike a round because the successive voices enter on different pitches.

NON NOBIS DOMINE

The students should learn this song as a unison melody. When they are very secure with it they may try it as a three-part canon as marked, with the second voice entering on the dominant, *so,* and the third on the low *do* if there are changed voices capable of this. If not, the third voice may enter on the same pitch as the first, the tonic.

This is precisely what happens in fugues. If students experience it, they will recognize it when they hear it.

Augmentation and Diminution

Sing "Brother John" as customarily notated, ♩♩♩♩ . Then without changing the tempo, sing it as it would sound if notated beginning with eighth notes: ♫♫♫ . This is "diminution." Try singing in two parts; half the class on the original notation, the other half on the diminished version. How many times did the group singing the "diminished" version have to sing the piece to end with the "original" group? (2).

Now maintaining the same tempo and conducting beat, have one group sing the melody, notated as ♩♩♩♩ against the group singing ♩♩♩♩ . This extending of each note to twice its original duration is called "augmentation." How many times did the "original" group have to sing to end with the augmented melody? (2).

Students should enter the terms "augmentation" and "diminution" on the music vocabulary page in their notebooks.

Sequence has been studied before, when preparing for the Haydn Cello Concerto in D Major. It should be reviewed here and perhaps "played with" in an instructive way.

Direction: "Sing Brother John"

Question: *The second time we sing "are you sleeping?" is the melody the same, similar to, or different from the first time?" (exactly the same)*

Question: *Is there any repeat in this song in which the tune is not the same? (No, each phrase repeats exactly.)*

Direction: Let's change this melody. Instead of an "exact repeat," lets sing a "sequence" one step higher after each phrase.

The result will be both fun and funny, but as a teaching device for "sequence," it works.

Direction: Sing the first two phrases of "America."

Question: *Is the second phrase the same, different from, or similar to the first?*

Answer: *The rhythm is the same. The first three notes are the same contour but in a higher place. The rest of the notes are different.*

Direction: The first three notes are a "sequence" to the first three notes of the first phrase. How would it sound if we continued the whole second phrase as a sequence?

Students try this

Generalization: Composers use sequences to give greater variety to compositions.

Changes in mode: minor to Major; I - V harmonic changes.

MAM'ZELLE ZIZI

This song is invaluable for two reasons, aside from the fact it is simply a charming Cajun folk song and a pleasure to sing. First, it has a regularly alternating I - V harmony with these chords clearly outlined in the melody; and second, the melody occurs first in minor, then in major and then again in minor. This is unusual in a folk song, but a very common technique in composed music. It is good preparation for recognizing mode shifts in larger works.

Once the song has been learned, the students' attention should be directed to the form and to the implied harmonization.

Question: *Are there phrases that are the same?* (1st, 3rd, and 7th are the same.) (4th and 8th are the same.)

Question: *Are any similar?* (5th is like the first, but higher. 6th is like the second, but higher.)

Question: *Is the piece in major or minor?* (Minor.) *The tonal center is on* la. *Then the tonic, i, would be* la. *What would V be?* (mi)

Direction: Find the i chord outlined in the melody:

Direction: Find the V chord outlined in the melody:

Let's sing this as a chord progression:

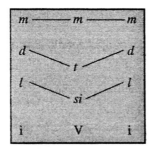

At this point have half the class sing the melody while the other half sings *la* or *mi* (i or V), making changes where needed. When they get to the 5th phrase they will immediately hear that something else is needed.

> Question: *Are these two phrases in minor?* (They will probably perceive that they are in Major, but if they do not, ask them to find a triad in the melody). *What are the notes of the triad?* (d-m-s.) *The tonic, I, in major; this section is in major. What will we have to sing to accompany it?* (*do* or *so.*)

Once the harmonization has been completely derived and marked into students' copies of the song, the accompaniment could be transferred to instruments and an arrangement of the piece created for xylophones, metalaphones, or whatever other instruments may be available.

At this point the subject of the D minor fugue may be introduced, sung, and memorized, in simplified form:

Question: *If we were to break this subject into smaller units, where do you think these breaks would occur? How could we organize this subject into smaller "motives"?*

How could we describe these "motives"? (One four-note descending scale pattern; two four-note ascending scale patterns.)

Sing the subject phrasing in such a way that the four-note motives are clear. Now have half the class sing the subject while the other half sustains the root of the V chord, *mi*. (Second space A.)

Information: Bach sometimes used one note called a "pedal point" in this way, sustaining it through a whole statement of the subject. Or sometimes he used one note alternating with the tune notes of the subject just to make it more interesting.

Question: *What did he do with this one?* (First Listening, first subject statement only.)

Answer: He alternated the *mi* with the melody notes of the subject.

The class should now be given the subject, fully notated, to sing and learn.

Question: *How many times does Bach state this subject in this fugue? Keep track by a simple scoring technique as you listen.*

Discussion: *How many did you find?* (Solicit answers from a number of students but do not signify whether they are right or wrong. There will be considerable divergence.) *I think we better hear it again and keep our tally together.*

(This provides opportunity for an immediate repetition of the recording and gives students a chance to correct their responses.) [There are 14.]

Question: *Were there any parts in the music that did not sound at all like the subject?* (Yes.) *These parts are called Episodes. They sometimes connect the different statements of the subject.*

Second Listening

For this complex piece students will be greatly aided if they are given a fairly concrete guide on which to pin their listening. They have determined by now that there are fourteen statements of the subject with episodes between some of them.

The listening chart given to them before this second listening experience should contain the information in the first column summarized for them. They will then listen to discover the entries for the other columns.

Students will listen to hear in what voice the subject occurs at each statement. The words high, middle, and low could be used, but this might be a good opportunity to teach:

soprano	high, female
alto	low, female
tenor	high, male
bass	low, male

and to relate these descriptions to the voices of the organ.

When the students have listened and written the voices into their charts they should be given time to discuss their responses before the teacher gives any needed corrections. If there is considerable disagreement, the students should listen again, following their voices guide placed on the board by the teacher.

Third Listening—Motives

How did Bach use the motives in this work? Where are they? What has he done with them when they are not being used within the complete subject?

- he sequenced them
- he used diminution
- he used the motives to accompany the subject.

The motives should be reviewed and sung before this listening.

Listening Chart

Work: The Fugue from the Toccata and Fugue in D minor
Composer: Johann Sebastian Bach   Dates: 1685–1750
Period: Baroque

Form	Voice	Other
1. Subject	Tenor	
2. Subject	Alto	
3. Subject	Soprano	4 note descending pattern, broken major chords
Episode		
4. Subject	Bass	
Episode		broken major chords
5. Subject	Tenor	in Major
Episode		clarion bells
6. Subject	Soprano	clarion bells
Episode		
7. Subject	Bass	overlapping fragmented "stretto" pedal point
8. Subject	Alto	overlapping fragmented "stretto" pedal point
9. Subject	Soprano	overlapping fragmented "stretto" pedal point
10. Subject	Tenor	broken major chords
Episode		
11. Subject	Alto	pedal on V
12. Subject	Soprano	
13. Subject	Bass	
Episode		pedal on I (do)
14. Subject		pedal on i (la)
Coda		4 note motives, diminution, fragments of subject

Fourth Listening—Pedal Point

We tried singing *mi*, the root of the Dominant under the subject. Let's try *la*.

Question: *Does Bach use a pedal note in this way in any of the subject state-ments?* (Yes.) *Where?* (In 7, 8, 10, 11, 12, 13, and 14. In some of these it appears as a trill, in some as the root of i (*la*) and in some as the root of V (*mi*).)

Fifth Listening—The Episodes; change of mode

To prepare for hearing what is happening in the episodes, students should practice singing a I V_6 I chord progression, both as chords and as broken chords. The Episodes are created from this simple harmony in the form of alternating arpeggios.

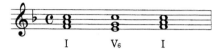

Question: *Is this work minor throughout?* (No.) *Where are there major sections?* (The Episodes, and at the fifth Subject statement.)

Sixth Listening

As a culminating activity for the study of this fugue the class could be divided into four or five groups, each charged with presenting the fugue in some clear way to the rest of the class. These ways could involve graphing or diagramming the form on large chart paper, organizing some sort of flow chart with different colors representing different voices showing each point of the music in a different way, or creating dance movement to illustrate the various parts of the fugue.

To add more variety to the presentations, recordings of transcriptions for orchestra, synthesizer, vocal groups, or brass ensembles could be used. All exist.

Students should be encouraged to critique one another's presentations in a positive way.

The D minor Fugue is a complex one. Should the teacher wish to use a simpler and shorter work for the students' initial exposure to this form, the *Little Fugue in G minor* is recommended.[1]

LISTENING STRATEGY 9

J.S. Bach, The *Brandenburg* Concerto No. 5, in D Major, First Movement

Background Information for the Teacher

The Baroque concerto or *concerto grosso* is different from later concertos in that it features a small group of instruments rather than one instrument. The *solo* parts called the *concertino* might involve two violins, or violin and oboe, or violin and flutes, or other combinations, accompanied by harpsichord. These *concertino* sections are alternated with *tutti* sections in which the whole orchestra plays.

---

[1] For a guide to this work, see Choksy, Abramson, Gillespie, *Teaching Music in the 20th Century* (Prentice Hall, 1986)

The usual form of the concerto grosso is in three movements, fast-slow-fast, with the first and last movements in *ritornello* form, the second in binary form.

A number of twentieth-century composers have returned to this form, among them Bloch, Hindemith, Piston, Stravinsky, and Bartok.

Ritornello Form

The word *ritornello* may be literally translated as "little return." In ritornello form the full orchestra (which may be only twenty or so players) plays the opening theme. This theme or part of it is played by the full orchestra each time it returns. In between the returns the small solo ensemble plays other themes, contrasting to the ritornello theme, or plays variations on the ritornello theme. The ritornello is played fully in the home key by the full orchestra in the first and last statements, but in the others may be incomplete and may be stated in other keys. Ritornello form might be outlined as:

1. tutti—ritornello, home key
2. solo ensemble, new musical material
3. tutti—ritornello, fragmented, new key
4. solo ensemble, new musical material
5. tutti—ritornello, fragmented, new key
6. solo ensemble, new musical material
7. tutti—ritornello, home key, full statement of ritornello theme.

The *Brandenburg* Concertos were written for a German nobleman. In this fifth of the six, Bach used the harpsichord for the first time as a solo instrument, giving it an elaborate cadenza-like section toward the end of the first movement. Previously the harpsichord had supplied only the basso continuo or other accompaniment part. The two other solo instruments in this concerto grosso are the violin and flute.

Preparation: *What do the students need to know before listening?*

The Harpsichord

The harpsichord will have been introduced briefly in the preceding year's study of keyboard instruments. It should be reviewed at this time, its plucking mechanism, its size and shape discussed, its characteristic sound experienced and compared to that of the piano.

Meter and Rhythm

The first movement of this work is in cut time [2]. This may be the students' first exposure to this meter. Some time should be spent introducing it and its usual signature, ¢.

The easiest way to do this is through movement. Using the circle dance "Sailing On the Ocean."

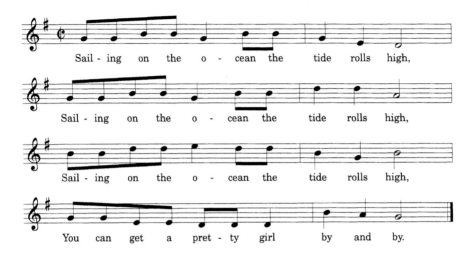

1. Have the students *step the beat.* (They will quite naturally step on *sail* and *o.*)
2. Ask them to clap the rhythm and sing it with rhythm syllables. They will perceive the rhythm as

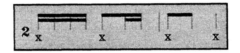

3. Question: *How many beats are you feeling in a measure; how is the music moving?* (In 2s.)
4. Now show them the correct notation of the first phrase without the meter sign.

5. *If there are only two beats in a measure, as you said, what kind of note must the beat note be? Where in this phrase is there one note on one beat?* (On high.)

What kind of note is on "high"? (Half note ♩.) This is our beat note, the lower number in the meter sign. How many beats did you feel in each measure? (2) Therefore our meter sign is:

$$2 \quad \text{or} \quad 2$$
$$\begin{matrix} ♩ & & 2 \end{matrix}$$

You remember that we had a way of showing $\frac{4}{4}$ without numbers, as "C." We have a similar way of showing $\frac{2}{2}$, ¢. It is called "ala breve" or "cut time."

Rhythm

The triplet, sung or spoken as *tri-o-la*, not previously encountered in notation, should also be taught in preparation for this work, in which it is used extensively. It may be introduced through any song in which it occurs:

HANDSOME MOLLY

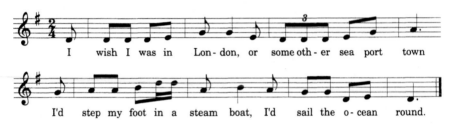

I   wish I was in   Lon-don, or   some oth-er sea port   town

I'd   step my foot in a   steam boat, I'd   sail the o-cean   round.

In song, triplets tend to occur as an exceptional figure in an otherwise straightforward duple setting. However, in compositions they may occur as the predominant rhythm throughout a section. To prepare for this some work with alternating duple and triple patterns may be helpful.

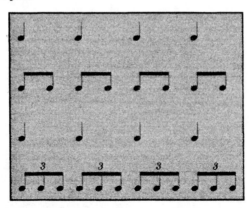

There are also suspensions across bar lines in this work, but they may be dealt with through the theme in which they occur.

The ritornello theme is highly instrumental in character. The range, encompassing as it does two octaves, necessitates that students sing some parts an octave lower than written (measures 3 and 6). The value of learning the theme as thoroughly as possible makes this added step worthwhile.

This theme may be taught by either a reading or a rote to note process. Once students have sung through it they should be led to analyze it. This will aid in memorization.

Question: *Which measures are the same?* (None.) *Which are similar?* (1 & 2 begin the same way; the last half of 3 is like the middle of 4 and the end of 6.) *Which measures have sequences?* (3, 4, 6; the last half of 7 is the same as the first half of 8 but in a higher place.) *Which measures have broken chords?* (1 & 2) *Which measures have scale passages?* (1, 5, 7, 8.)

First Listening:

Listen to the complete first movement to identify the form.

Listen to discover how many times this theme occurs either fully or in part, played by the full orchestra, and to decide whether there is a pattern in its recurrence.

There should be free and open discussion after this listening. Students will probably have identified the nine tutti sections correctly.

Question: *What was happening the rest of the time?* (Fewer instruments playing, some solo passages)

Information: This form is called ritornello because the principal theme, played by the full orchestra, keeps returning. In between its returns a small ensemble of solo instruments plays other themes. The work is called a *concerto grosso*, and this particular concerto grosso is one of six written by Bach, called the *Brandenburg* Concertos.

Second Listening

Listen to the full movement to identify the instrumentation.

At this time the listening chart could be distributed. As an aid to the students, the *form* column could be given. They have already discussed it.

The focus of this listening will be particularly on the solo sections, since in the *tutti* sections the strings always play the theme.

Third Listening: The First Solo Section

The interplay between the flute and violin in this small segment is quite lovely and the imitation of one voice by the other is interesting.

Teaching Procedure

Question: *What can we do with a simple scale passage to make it interesting?* Some possible answers might be:

- vary it rhythmically
- ornament it
- change instruments (timbre)
- change dynamics
- do it in higher and lower places
- have voices imitate each other in canon
- shift to a faster or slower tempo

Students may have still other suggestions. These should be listed on the chalk board.

Information: *In the first solo section, Bach uses the descending scale: d^1 t l s f m r_.* (Students sing the scale.) *Listen to the beginning.* (Teacher should play only the first three bars, only the piano.)

Which of your suggestions did Bach employ to vary this scale passage? (He varied the rhythm, he had the second voice imitate the first.)

Listen to this short section of the recording to hear whether he did anything else on your list. (Play this short segment on the recording.) (He changed the timbre; the thin tone of the flute is followed by the richer tone of the violin, and he used a softer dynamic level than in the tutti section).

What did Bach not do that is on our list? (ornament it, change the tempo, possibly other suggestions from the students' list)

Information: *For the second part of this solo section Bach used an ascending scale pattern with a repeated note in the middle.*

Direction: *Let's go through your list and try various ways of giving this scale passage some variety.*

Student improvisations on this scale will not all work, but the purpose is not to produce a beautiful composition, it is to experiment with the various ways available to Bach for varying a theme.

Direction: *Listen to find out how Bach varied this theme.* Play only the first solo section.

- He used sequences—each entrance a step higher.
- He ornamented the scale using a triplet figure:

- He had the two instruments alternate, changing in the middle of the scale pattern at the repeated notes: violin *ti d'r'm'*; flute *r m f s*, thus changing the timbre.

At this point students should be given the notation of the first solo section theme and should listen to the recording from the beginning of the piece to the end of this section.

Fourth Listening: Change of Mode

Question: *Most of this movement is clearly in major. Where does it shift briefly to the minor mode?* (At the 4th and 5th return.)

Fifth Listening

This listening could be relatively unstructured. If a modern orchestra recording has been used previously, this might be a good point at which to listen to one featuring original instruments. Discussion following could focus on the timbral effects of the two kinds of instrumental sound.

Listening Chart

Work: Brandenburg Concerto No. 5 in D Major, first movement

Composer: Johann Sebastian Bach   **Dates: 1685–1750**

Period: Baroque   **Form: Concerto Grosso (ritornello)**

Form	Instruments	Theme(s)	mode	dynamics
1. Tutti	strings	full ritornello theme	Major	*f*
Concertino	flute, violin	new theme introduced		softer
(solo ensemble)	harpsichord	imitation, triplets, key change		
2. Tutti	strings	rit. theme, only to m. 2		*f*
Concertino	flute, violin	rit theme, m. 3 used as a		softer
	harpsichord	motive, varied		
3. Tutti	strings	rit. theme, begun at end of m. 2		*f*
Concertino	violin, flute	descending patterns by violin		softer
	harpsichord	and flute		
4. Tutti	strings	rit. theme, begun at end of m. 2	minor	*f*
				softer
Concertino	harpsichord	variations on rit. theme m. 3	minor with	
	flute, violin		return to	
			Major	
5. Tutti	strings	rit. theme begun at m. 6	Major	*f*
Concertino	flute, violin	new theme, flute on	minor	*pp*
	harpsichord	descending triads, trills at end		
6. Tutti	strings	rit. theme from the beginning	Major	*f*
Concertino	flute, violin	return to first concertino		softer
	harpsichord	theme		
7. Tutti	strings	rit. theme from the beginning		*f*
Concertino	violin, harpsichord	variation on rit. theme		softer
	flute			
8. Tutti	strings	theme begins at m. 3		*f*
Concertino	violin & flute;	begins with variation of		
	harpsichord on scale	concertino theme 1. Long		
	accompaniment,	cadenza-like section based		
	followed by	on previously introduced		
	harpsichord solo	material		
9. Tutti	strings	full & complete statement of ritornello theme in original key		*f*

As inconceivable as it may seem today, Bach was neither well known nor widely performed in his own time. He viewed his music simply as a craft. It had been passed down to him by his father, his grandfather, and his great-grandfather, all of whom had been musicians. He in turn passed it down to four of his sons. His phenomenal outpouring of music was largely forgotten until Felix Mendelssohn revived the *St. Matthew Passion* in 1829 in Berlin and began a process of rediscovery that has not ended to this day.

Bach spent his life as a church musician. Most of his creative output was in the service of the church.

LISTENING STRATEGY 10

George Frideric Handel, *The Water Music*

George Frideric Handel (1658–1759), born in Germany in the same year as Bach, chose a very different path. At the age of twenty-one he went to Italy for three years, where he composed highly acclaimed operas in the Italian style. He returned briefly to Germany, but after one trip to England, for the production of his opera *Rinaldo*, he returned to England for fifty years, from 1712 to 1759, even Anglicizing his name, and was considered to be England's most important composer. He was supported by Queen Anne and, after her death, by King George I with an annual stipend of £400, in those days a substantial sum.

The music he composed was for the entertainment of his royal patrons—operas, oratorios, and incidental music for festive occasions. Even The *Messiah*, which one tends to think of as the epitome of religious music, was written not for performance in church but as a theater piece.

In all, Handel composed 39 operas, 25 oratorios, and numerous instrumental works. It is a mark of the degree of respect accorded to him by his adopted country that when he died he was buried in Westminster Abbey.

A characteristic piece by Handel is recommended here for study: The *Water Music* Suite.

Background Information for the Teacher

Water parties were a form of entertainment much enjoyed by the nobility in Handel's time. The music of these suites was composed at the King's request for a particular water party during which King George I and the royal family and members of the court were rowed up the Thames on barges while fifty musicians performed for them on an adjoining barge.

The music consists of twenty-two short pieces organized into three suites related only by the fact that they are all in dance forms and that, within each suite, they are in the same key. It is probable that some of these pieces were not even originally composed for these particular suites, but were merely pressed into service for them by Handel.

Form

The Baroque suite is a loosely organized collection of old dances put together in such a way that faster and slower tempos alternate, all performed in the same key. They generally consist of:

Allemande: a moderately slow duple with much subdivision of the beat.
Courante: a moderately slow triple, used as a companion to the Allemande. In the Courante the subdivisions of the beat may sometimes lead the listener to feel the meter as compound (1 2 3 4 5 6) rather than simple (1 2 3 4 5 6).
Sarabande: a slow, sedate triple meter with a slight feeling of accent on the second beat of each measure (1 2 3)
Gigue: a fast, lively movement in 6/8.
Minuet: a straightforward triple in a walking tempo. Two minuets are often put together within a suite to create an A B A form.

Numerous other dance forms may be used in suites—pavane, bourée, rigadon, gavotte, passepied, polonaise, gailliard, hornpipe. There is, as well, usually an overture. The Bach *French* Suites are examples of suites following this strict form. The *Water Music* is a good example through which to introduce suites because it is tuneful and lively. However, it does not follow the suite form as rigidly as some other works.

The three *Water Music* suites include an overture, five minuets, two bourées, two hornpipes, a rigadon, and two gigues. In addition there are some movements designated only by tempo marking, lentment, adagio, andante, and allegro. These movements are clearly of dance character also, even though they have not been designated as such.

For purposes of these lessons, one movement from the Suite in F Major (HWV 348) has been singled out: the third movement, marked Allegro. Andante-Allegro da capo.[2]

---

[2] These are following the order given in the edition by Chrysander, vol. 47, Leipzig, 1886, as recorded by the English Consort, under conductor Trevor Pinnock, Archiv Produktion No.410525-4. A-H and by the Amsterdam Baroque Orchestra, conductor Tom Koopman, ERATO 4509-91716-2.

The *Water Music,* Suite in F Major (HWV 348) by George Frideric Handel
Third Movement, Allegro-Andante-Allegro da Capo

What Do Students Need to Know Before Listening?

Compositional Devices

Handel made extensive use of sequences in the *Water Music*. Students have previously identified and worked with sequences when they studied the Haydn Cello Concerto in D Major, Op. 10 and the Bach Fugue in D minor. At this point they should be encouraged to use sequence as a way of extending a musical idea. This can be done in an extremely structured way:

1. Teacher: *Read the rhythm. One, Ready, Read!*

2. *Now sing the first measure in solfa:*

│ ⊓ │

d   d   r   d

3. *Use sequences to improvise measures two and three. End the phrase as a question.* (on *so, ti, re,* or *fa*) *You may make your sequence move either higher or lower.*

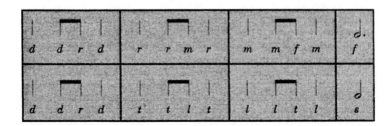

Or it can be completed in a less structured manner if the students are sufficiently prepared:

Teacher:

1. *Compose a four-phrase rhythm in 3/4 meter in A A B A form.*
2. *Add a melody using any of the notes of the major scale.*
3. *Use sequence in some way in the B phrase.*

Meter

There is a shift from $\frac{3}{4}$ in the allegro section to $\frac{4}{4}$ in the andante, as well as a change in tempo. The singing game "Coffee Grows on White Oak Trees" has the same shift of meter and tempo as well as the same da capo form. It provides an excellent preparation for these aspects in the *Water Music*. Students should sing this song, conducting it in triple and duple and should perform the dance.

At this point the rhythm of the allegro could be placed on the board for students to read and memorize:

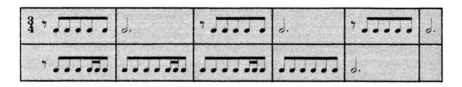

In a subsequent lesson the staff notation of the melody could be distributed and sung. The first phrase consists only of the notes of the tonic chord, d-m-s, and the second is a series of descending sequence patterns.

Students should identify the tonic chord and the sequences in the melody.

First Listening

The students may listen to the andante at this point, focusing on the instrumentation. The rhythmic motive  is stated by the brass and echoed by the strings throughout the movement.

This could be indicated on the students' listening charts.

Second Listening

The syncopated rhythm in the finale of the allegro should be introduced before this listening. It is a pattern students may not have encountered previously.

While the ♪ ♩ ♪ pattern is fairly common in songs the syncopation pattern found here is a bit more complex and is rarely found in vocal music. It is further complicated by the fact that it is in triple meter:

Procedure

To prepare for these rhythmic patterns, one possible process would be to begin with a three-beat pattern of separated eighth notes on the chalkboard: ♪♪♪♪♪♪.

Teacher: tap and say: *One, Ready, Read!*

Students: *ti ti ti ti ti ti* (tapping eights lightly on desk while saying).

Teacher: *I'm going to tie some of these notes together. Continue tapping all the eighth notes, but where two are tied together say them as "ta" and hold the sound through the two taps.*

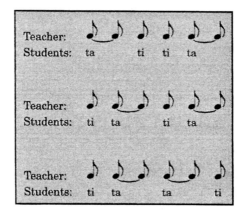

Further practice with syncopation in 3/4 could be given via rhythm-erase exercises and through having students use these patterns in rhythmic improvisation and composition.
The syncopated melody from the allegro could now be sung:

And students could listen to the allegro to find the syncopated section.

Third Listening

The students should now listen to the entire allegro-andante-allegro. It is about seven minutes in length. The focus of this listening is to identify the overall form (A-B-A) and to be able to describe the ways in which the andante is different from the allegro (meter, tempo, mode, dynamics, lyricism of the melodic line). Not all these differences may be discerned by the students in one hearing, but those they do perceive should be listed for later reference.

Fourth Listening

The notation of the andante may now be distributed to the students and sung.

Note that although Handel did not change the key signature, he did actually change the key from F major to the relative minor, D.

Students should listen again to determine the ways in which the andante provides contrast between the two statements of the allegro.

Fifth Listening

If a standard symphonic performance of this work was initially used with the students, they should now hear it on original instruments, as Handel might have heard it.

Listening Chart

Any chart used for this work can be a simple one, focusing broadly on instumentation, meter, mode, tempo, and dynamics.

Listening Chart				
Work: *Water Music* Suite in F Major (HWV 348), Third Movement				
Composer: George Frideric Handel			Dates: 1658–1759	
Period: Baroque			Form: A B A	
Movement	Instrumentation	Tempo & Dynamics	Mode	Meter
Allegro	brass and strings	fast tempo, loud "echos"	Major	3/4
	echoing each other	a bit softer		
	throughout			
Andante	woodwinds	slow, soft, singing quality	minor	4/4
	& harpsichord			
Allegro	as first statement	fast, loud	Major	3/4
	alternating brass			
	& strings			

Chapter 7

Experiences in Directed Listening: Music of Schubert and Brahms

BACKGROUND INFORMATION FOR THE TEACHER

The nineteenth-century saw massive changes in social structure and in the arts. The French Revolution was followed by a long period of unrest in France and by political upheaval in Germany, Austria, and Italy.

Artists, musicians and poets were prominent among those striving for political, religious, and personal freedom. It was an age in which freedom of expression was valued above all. The perception of artists as rebels and bohemians had its origins in this milieu.

The term "Romantic" was taken from literature, (this being the time of the great Romantic poets Byron, Keats and Shelley) and applied to all the arts of the period.

Numerous changes took place during the nineteenth-century that contributed to Romanticism. One result of the political instability was that class barriers, already diminished during Beethoven's lifetime, were further eroded. There was now the clear possibility of upward mobility of the lower and middle classes. Composers mixed socially with aristocrats. No longer were they considered servants.

With the new freedoms came a veritable explosion of public concerts and concert venues. Concerts were moved once and for all from the private salons of the nobility to commercial public concert halls. Every good-sized town had such a hall with its symphony orchestra, supported by middle-class patrons, merchants, bankers, lawyers, and the like.

The Industrial Revolution brought with it as well cheaper and more responsive instruments. Valves were added to brass instruments. The piano was given a cast iron frame and thicker strings. Woodwinds, which had previously had difficulty playing in tune in all keys and playing at all in some keys were revolutionized by the invention of the axle-mounted key. Range and dexterity were improved in all wind instruments. The orchestra was increased in size and content, with additional wind instruments and percussion and greater numbers in the string section.

The music composed during this period tended to reflect the spirit of freedom. Tempo was less rigid with "rubato," (robbed time) a frequent tempo indication. Melody was all important, emotional, climactic, and sensuous. In harmony, composers experimented with new chords and chord progressions and made greater use of chromaticism. The capabilities of the new and improved instruments led to more attention being paid by composers to orchestral timbres and effects and to the greater dynamic range now possible.

Forms developed in the Classical and Baroque Eras were still followed, but much more loosely than in earlier times. Some composers began to write "program music," music designed to illustrate a story or poem, for which the only "form" was the text.

Franz Schubert, born in 1797, might be viewed as the first wholly "Romantic" composer, and the ten-year period between 1803 and 1813 saw the birth of seven other great composers in the Romantic Style: Robert Schumann, Frederick Chopin, Felix Mendelssohn, Franz Liszt, Hector Berlioz, Richard Wagner, and Guiseppi Verdi. This style of composition continued with the music of Johannes Brahms (1833–97) and came to its culmination in the Romantic Expressionism of Gustav Mahler (1860–1911) and Richard Strauss (1864–1949).

What Do Students Need to Know to Approach the Music of This Period?

If students have not yet compared the sounds of early instruments with those of the nineteenth and twentieth Centuries they should do so at this time. There are numerous recordings available of Mozart and Haydn symphonies and concerti using early instruments—horns without valves for example—which may be compared in sound with the same works performed on modern instruments. Other aspects of the period that could be investigated by students include the rise of the virtuoso performer—Franz Liszt and Nicolo Paganini were prime examples—and the increased importance given to the orchestral conductor. The piano went during this period from being a drawing room or salon instrument of subdued tone to being "grand"—huge in size and sound. Students could read and report to the class on any of these developments.

The works of two composers have been chosen as illustrative of the Romantic style—Schubert who was the earliest "Romantic," and Brahms, whose music was avowedly classical in style but is fully romantic in its melodies and lush harmonies and orchestration.

Franz Schubert (1797–1828) was profoundly influenced by the music of Beethoven. His existence was the picture of what might be viewed as bohemian. He had no regular employment, being dependent on occasional teaching and publication to eke out a meager existence. He was, however, surrounded by a group of devoted friends, the "Schubertians," musicians, artists, writers, and music lovers who recognized and supported his genius. Schubert composed numerous operas, symphonies, sonatas, and chamber works; but he is chiefly remembered for the more than 600 songs he created in the short 31 years he lived.

Deeply influenced by the poetry of his time, Schubert established the *lied* ("song," plural—*lieder*—pronounced "leader") as an important form. For this he chose poetry he considered to have artistic merit on its own and worked to present melody, accompaniment, and text as one interrelated whole.

He brought the song as an artistic musical form to a level never reached before, and paved the way for later important composers of lieder such as Robert Schumann and Hugo Wolf.

Schubert's songs are of two basic types:

- strophic, in which the tune is the same for each verse of the poetry
- through-composed, in which the music changes as the story unfolds in the text in such a way that the drama of the text is described and underlined by the music.

Numerous Schubert songs are performable by students in fifth grade and above. *"Hedge Roses," "The Wanderer," "Ave Maria"* and many others are suitable in range and no more difficult than far less worthy music in commercial school series. Their inclusion in any upper elementary or secondary choral curriculum is recommended.

LISTENING STRATEGY 11

Franz Schubert, "Die Forelle" (The Trout)

The song chosen for inclusion here is "Die Forelle" (The Trout). It lies somewhere between a strophic and a through-composed song in that the melody and accompaniment change to underline the text at the dramatic climax of the song, but otherwise are the same for each verse.

THE TROUT

1. A stream let clear and sun - ny with rip - ples all a -
2. A fish - er with his an - gle stood al - so on the

bout was once the bath for bon - ny, for gen - tle lit - tle
shore, Hard try- ing to en - tan - gle the fish - es more and

trout. On shore I stood ob - ser - ving with ex - quit- site de -
more I thought if clear the wat - er con - tin - ues here a -

light. For such a hap - py creat - ure, it was a cheer - ful
bout, The wretch will ne - ver cap - ture my bon - ny lit - tle

sight. For such a hap - py creat- ure, it was a cheer- ful
trout. You'll ne - ver catch, you vil - lan, my bon- ney lit - tle

sight.   3. But then the bus - y fish - er,
trout.

to get his prey for spite he madfe the wa - ter

mud - dy, And them with out de - lay, So quick the rod had

dart- ed He cap - tured, he hooked the fish so sweet. I

saw with sad- den'd feel - ing, The cheat - ed and the cheat, I

saw with sad - den'd feel - ing the cheat- ed and the cheat.

The overall form is A A B A, with the B section presenting the dramatic climax.

The poem, written by the German poet Christian Friedrich Daniel Schubert, is told in the words of someone walking by a stream enjoying the beauty of nature. In the clear, sparkling water the stroller spies a darting, playful trout. As the observer watches, a fisherman appears and attempts to catch the trout. The fisherman's efforts are at first unsuccessful, the water being clear and the trout able to see the line. The fisherman takes a stick and stirs up the water, making it muddy, so that the trout cannot see the line, and through this trick catches the trout. The last line of the song expresses the observer's dismay on regarding "the cheated and the cheat." A simple story, simply and beautifully expressed in song.

Teaching Procedure

The teacher should present the song as an artistic whole, singing it unaccompanied for the class, modeling phrasing, tempo, and dynamics. The class may have music and text (in English) in front of them for this initial experience.

The teacher should next focus attention on the text and lead students to discuss the way in which the melody lends dramatic impact to the text.

The song may then be taught to the students by a rote, rote-note or reading method, depending on the capabilities and background of the group.

When the song is being sung with accuracy and good musical expression, the piano accompaniment may be played. It could be played separately first and opinions elicited from the class as to what it is picturing (the motion of the stream, the muddying of the water). The students should come to the conclusion that piano and voice are equal partners in setting the mood and telling the story. This is a fundamental characteristic of lieder.

When the students are performing the song well with accompaniment they should hear it as performed by some of the great twentieth-century lieder singers such as Dietrich Fisher-Dieskau and Elizabeth Schwartzkoff. Since these performances will be in German, it is recommended that the German text be given to the students. They could later be led to sing it in the original language themselves. Older students are capable of singing in languages other than English, and enjoy doing so.

The students knowledge of theory could be extended through an analysis of the consonant harmonies Schubert used to picture the idyllic country scene (I, IV, and V for the most part) and the dissonant ones he used to indicate the muddying of the water.

When studying the music of Mozart and Haydn students have worked with I, IV, and V triads in root position and in inversion. With the music of Beethoven they have added secondary chords and common chord progressions and cadences. For music of the Romantic period they need to extend to thicker harmonies and less obvious progressions. They might, for example isolate and sing the chords used to illustrate the muddying of the water in "The Trout":

Played low in the bass clef:

When the students have learned, analyzed and listened to the Schubert song they may be introduced to the chamber music setting he made of this lied.

FORM: THEME AND VARIATIONS

LISTENING STRATEGY 12

Schubert Quintet, Op. 114, "The Trout," Fourth Movement.

First Listening

Since the students are already familiar with the song the first statement of the theme may be presented without further preparation.

Schubert liked this melody so much that he used it again in a Quintet. How many instruments are in a quintet? (5.) *Listen to see what the instruments are.* (Play only the first section, the first complete statement of the melody.) Students should be able to identify the instruments as:

- violin
- viola
- cello
- double bass

Which of these instruments is unusual in chamber music? (the bass)

But we have listed only four instruments. Where is the fifth? And what is the fifth? (Play the recording again, continuing through the first variation.)

Yes, the fifth instrument is the piano. How did Schubert extend the melody? (He had the first section repeated.)

Second Listening

Introduce the cello part. Have students sing the two parts together, cello and violin, and then softly sing the cello part with the recording. By singing inner voices we become more conscious of them and capable of hearing more than just the "tune."

THE TROUT, CELLO PART

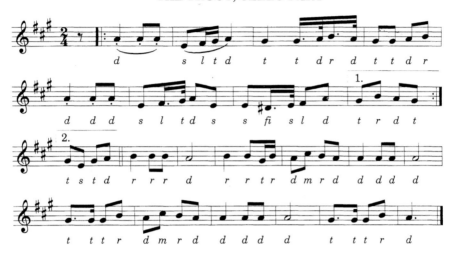

Only the theme statement (first section) should be played in this lesson.

Third Listening

Introduce the bass part as written in the bass clef and have students sing it, first separately, then with the cello and violin parts. Treble voices will sound odd on this line, but singing it will lead to hearing it. Play the first section of the movement, having the students softly sing the bass line with it.

Fourth Listening

Students should be made aware that not all instruments read from treble or bass clefs. The viola plays from a clef in which middle C is on the third line.

C CLEF ON STAFF

Middle C

F   G   A   B   C   D   E   F   G

VIOLA PART

Once the class has learned the viola part they should sing it with the other parts if they are vocally secure enough to do so, or in unison with the recording if they are not able to sing in so many parts.

With the theme now thoroughly learned students are ready to study the variations.

Music has some things that hold it together—give it unity—and some things that keep it interesting, that give it variety. Unity and variety are two very important qualities in all music. In theme and variation form, it is the theme itself that provides the unity. The composer plays with the theme in ways that vary it— that change it.

What are some of the ways we can vary a theme? (List responses on the chalk-board.) *We could:*

- change the rhythm:
  - repeated notes
  - smooth to jagged
  - augment
  - diminish
- change the meter
- change the mode: major to minor or minor to major
- put the theme in different voices; vary the timbre
- put it in different keys
- change the dynamics
- change the tempo
- change the accompaniment—put the accompaniment in different voices
- do parts of it in canon
- state the theme backward; upside down
- extend parts of the theme by using sequences

These and any other suggestions for varying a theme should be tried with a familiar song. "Brother John" and "Go Tell Aunt Rhody" work well for such experimentation, however any simple, small range, 4-phrase song will work as well. The objective is the experimentation. The result need not be beautiful.

Here is the notation of the first two phrases of the "Trout" theme. Compose a two phrase variation. You may use any of the above ideas or any other idea for variation you may think of. The only rule is that we must be able to find the tune somewhere in your variation.

In the subsequent lesson student composed variations should be performed and discussed.

Fifth Listening

At this time the entire theme and variation movement could be played and students led to fill out a listening chart.

Variation 1: Theme: piano. Strings play the "rippling stream" notes. Use of ornamentation, trills, and broken chords in accompaniment.

Variation 2: Theme: viola & cello. Piano: chords. Violin: broken triads, scales.

Variation 3: Theme: cello & double bass. Piano: fast moving accompaniment. The other strings play a rhythmic accompaniment that could be followed by the class from notation.

Listening Chart

Work: _____

Composer: _____ Period: _____

Instrumentation: _____ Form: _____

Theme: (notated by the students)

Form	Instrument(s)	How the Theme is changed	Instrument Characteristics
Theme statement			
Var 1			
Var 2			
Var 3			
Var 4			
Var 5			
Theme statement			

Characteristics of the Period: _____

_____

In the first three variations the principal means of varying the theme has been through timbre—having different instruments play the theme.

Variation 4: Change to minor. The theme is recognizable only at the beginning—it is obscured, but if one "thinks it" in minor it fits. It is implied rather than obviously stated. The texture is thick, the dynamic level loud. Use of triplets.

Variation 5: The cello plays the melody. The theme is fragmented. The mode is predominantly major with hints of minor tonality. Change of key at the beginning of this variation. Piano on chords. Piano not playing in some places.

Final theme restatement: Theme. Violin phrases 1-2, cello repeats, violin phrases 3-5, cello repeats 3-4, violin and cello together on 5.

To discover all the information in the above chart students may have to listen to the entire movement several times in the course of the next three or four lessons.

Because there are only five instruments this might be a good example for which to have students see a score. Even if they follow the theme from one instrument to another in only one variation (no. 2 for example) they will have learned something about score reading.

LISTENING STRATEGY 13

Johannes Brahms Symphony No. 4 in E Major, Op. 98, Fourth Movement.

Information for the Teacher

Johannes Brahms (1833–97) was born in Hamburg, Germany, the son of a bass player in the local theatre orchestra. He was given lessons on violin, cello and horn by his father, and on piano and in composition from the other teachers in the city as a child. In his twenties he met composer Robert Schumann, who was deeply impressed by him and who brought him to the attention of the musical world.

Brahms held a succession of minor musical posts in Hamburg before gravitating, like Beethoven before him, to Vienna where he spent the remainder of his life.

The music of Brahms is stylistically in a direct line from that of Beethoven, Schubert, and Schumann. He rarely employed the chromaticism and modulation exhibited in the music of his contemporaries Liszt and Wagner. He wrote no "tone poems."

His music tended to follow quite strictly classical forms. However, within these forms he offered beautiful lyrical melodies, rich harmonies, and interesting new combinations of rhythms.

His four symphonies were all composed during the last twenty years of his life. They are powerful works of heroic proportions.

The Music

The work offered for study here is the fourth movement, marked *allegro energico e passionato* of the Symphony No. 4 in E minor, Op. 98.

It is in a form much favored by Baroque composers, the passacaglia, a kind of theme and variations. For this theme, Brahms borrowed from Bach's Cantata No. 150, "Unto Thee, O Lord, I Lift Up My Soul."

Students have studied theme and variations previously in Mozart's "Ah Vous Dirai-je Maman" and Schubert's "Trout" Quintet. The passacaglia form is a stricter one. In Baroque compositions, of which Bach's C minor Passacaglia is an excellent example, the theme is always in the bass, and the variations are essentially counter melodies. It is also always in triple metre and is 8 measures in length.

Brahms' passacaglia consists of an eight measure, triple meter theme, followed by a set of thirty variations, each also exactly eight measures in length. His only departures from the strict Baroque form are in the shifting of the theme from the bass to other voices and in a metre change from 3/4 to 3/2 which has the effect of rhythmically augmenting one section.

Teaching Procedure

The theme may be introduced to the students first as a simple E-minor scale passage:

This is the theme as Bach wrote it.

Brahms creates immediate interest through the insertion of one chromatic tone into this scale:

Students should sing, memorize, and notate this theme, after which they may be led to discuss ways in which it could be varied. Suggestions might include:

How could we vary this rhythmically?
- use repeated notes
- use syncopation.
- change the meter
- use uneven or jogged rhythms

How could we vary it melodically?
- put notes between the melody notes
- add counter melodies
- have the melody performed by different instruments

How could we vary it harmonically?
- minor to Major
- use thick chords
- use broken chords
- use canonic imitation

All student suggestions should be attempted vocally or instrumentally with the theme.

First Listening

Play only the theme. *How would you describe this theme? We learned it as a simple scale, does it still sound like a simple scale?* (No. It has a strong forceful character not hinted at by merely singing the theme.)

What gives it this forcefulness? (The harmonies and the instrumentation. The use of brass gives it a fanfare-like sound).

Let's examine the bass line.

What is its direction? (Descending, in contrary motion to the theme.)

Second Listening

Play the theme statement. Students sing the bass line with the recording, changing octaves where necessary.

Third Listening

Distribute a listening chart on which students:
- notate the theme from memory
- enter the title, composer, and dates
- list the form

Listen to the theme and the first two variations (this takes us about three minutes into the work). Fill out the sections on the listening chart as to the instrument in which the theme occurs and what is happening in other voices.

Discuss which of the student-suggestions for variation were incorporated by Brahms.

Fourth Listening

Variations 12 through 15 are in 3/2. This is, in effect, augmentation of the original passacaglia theme. Students should review the principle of augmentation and be introduced to 3/2 meter.

Teaching Procedure for Augmentation and the Half Note as the Beat Note

Have students learn "Rise Up O Flame."

How is the music moving? (In 3s.) The beat note is ♩ ; the meter $\frac{3}{\rho}$ or $\frac{3}{4}$. *If we wanted each of these notes to sound twice as long how could we show them?*

Sing as newly notated. *How is it moving?* (Still in 3s.) *What is the beat note now?*

(The half note). *What would the meter sign be?* $\left(\frac{3}{\rho} \text{ or } \frac{3}{2}.\right)$ When we stretch a rhythm out—make each note twice as long—we are augmenting it. (Vocabulary Term: Augmentation.)

This should perhaps be followed by reading and performing a song originally composed in $\frac{3}{2}$. The following eight-part canon is a possibility.

J. C. Stierlein (XVIII C.)

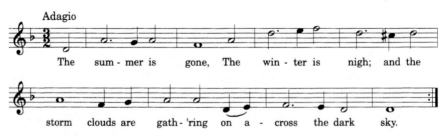

This must all be then related back to the Brahms' passacaglia theme. Returning to the original notation, how would it look, rhythmically augmented? It could be:

But instead, Brahms chooses to use the stretched out measures to present a syncopated rhythm—the theme on off-beats:

Now listen to Variations 12 through 15. Three of the four are in major. Fill in the listening chart for these variations.

Fifth Listening

Listen to variations 16 through 30 and the coda. These are strongly rhythmic and, like the first eleven, dramatic in character.
Fill in the listening chart for these variations.

Sixth Listening

Listen to the entire fourth movement (about ten minutes in length). Add any further comments as desired to the listening chart.
For teachers, this composition is shown here in final chart form.

Listening Chart

Work: Symphony No. 4 in E minor, Op. 90, 4th movement (Passacaglia)

Composer: Johannes Brahms   **Dates: 1833–1897**

Period: Romantic   **Form: Passacaglia**

Form	Theme Instrument	Accompaniment	Mode	Tempo	Dynamics
Theme	brass & ww	chords	minor	energetic	*forte*
Var 1	pizzicato violins	horns & timpani	minor	energetic	*decrescendo*
Var 2	pizzicato cellos	oboe countermelody	minor	energetic	*mp*
Var 3	woodwinds	brasses/timpani roll	minor	energetic	*forte*
Var 4	basses	lyrical countermelody in violins	minor	original tempo/legato	*forte*
Var 5	cellos & basses	violin countermelody continued	minor	legato	*forte*
Var 6	basses (legato)	violins continue variation	minor	legato	*crescendo*
Var 7	basses	violin descending melody, dotted rhythm	minor	original tempo	*forte*
Var 8	basses	fast notes in violin	minor	original tempo	*decrescendo*
Var 9	low strings	faster notes in violin, descending flute	minor	original tempo	*subito forte, sub piano*
Var 10	low strings	chords strings/woodwinds	minor	original tempo	*piano*
Var 11	violins	flutes descending chromatic scale	minor	original tempo	*pianissimo*
Var 12	legato flute theme var	strings	minor	3/2 slower, augmented	*piano, decrescendo*
Var 13	clarinet & oboe	low strings	Major	3/2 slower, augmented	*pianissimo*
Var 14	trombone slow chords	strings-horn	Major	3/2 slower, augmented	*piano*
Var 15	oboe	slow chords in strings	Major	3/2 slower, augmented	*ritardando*
Var 16	brass & woodwinds	high violins on descending scale	minor	original tempo	*fortissimo*
Var 17	woodwinds	strings on tremolo	minor	original tempo	*mezzo-forte*
Var 18	horns & high woodwinds	ascending line	minor	original tempo	*crescendo-forte*
Var 19	strings, woodwinds	chords in strings	minor	original tempo	*forte*
Var 20	strings	brass	minor	original tempo	*forte*
Var 21	violins	horns punctuating	minor	original tempo	*fortissimo*
Var 22	strings	staccato woodwinds & strings	minor	original tempo	*subito piano*
Var 23	horns	strings	minor	original tempo	*subito forte*
Var 24	high violins	brass on I & V (la & mi)	minor	original tempo	*fortissimo*
Var 25	high tremolo violins	chords in brass	minor	original tempo	*fortissimo*
Var 26	horns	oboes & violas	minor	original tempo	*subito piano*
Var 27	woodwinds	strings	minor	original tempo	*piano*
Var 28	high woodwinds	strings	minor	original tempo	*piano*
Var 29	flute	pizzicato strings	minor	original tempo	*piano*
Var 30	cellos & violins	timpani rolls	minor	slower	*subito forte*
Coda	brass & woodwinds		minor	faster	*fortissimo*
	trombones	staccato	minor	faster	*fortissimo*
	violins		minor		*piano-crescendo*
	woodwinds	ascending melody	minor		*fortissimo*
	full orchestra	chords	minor		*fortissimo*

Chapter 8   *

Music of the Impressionist Period and Early Twentieth-Century

BACKGROUND INFORMATION FOR THE TEACHER

The end of the nineteenth-century saw a sharp movement away from prescribed Germanic forms and harmonic progressions, brought about principally by the music of one composer, Claude Debussy (1862–1918).

Debussy was born in a small village on the outskirts of Paris and lived most of his life in that city. He attended the Paris Conservatoire from age eleven, and won the Prix de Rome upon graduation, entitling him to three years study in Rome. On a trip to Moscow he discovered Rimsky-Korsakov and Borodin, who clearly left their mark on his music.

However, the strongest influence on Debussy's music was not other music, but the society of contemporary artists and writers in Paris at the turn of the century. Poets Mallarmé and Verlaine, painters Manet, Monet and Renoir were among his friends and colleagues. All stressed imagery rather than description, impression rather than graphic portrayal in their art.

Debussy wrote:

I desire for music that freedom of which it is capable perhaps to a greater degree than any other art, as it is not confined to an exact reproduction of nature, but only to the mysterious affinity between Nature and Imagination.[1]

---

[1] Leon Vallas, *Claude Debussy: His Life and Works* (London, 1983) p. 85.

LISTENING STRATEGY 14

Claude Debussy, Nuages (from Nocturnes)

First Listening

Because of the nature of this music, because it was composed to offer "impressions," the best place to start is probably with the music itself. Allow the students to hear it—knowing its title: "Clouds"; it is short, only eight minutes in length. Encourage discussion after this listening. Place descriptive words supplied by the students on the chalkboard. Then show a print of a painting from the same period. These are available in most art galleries. Vincent Van Gogh's "Blue Skies and White Clouds" (1890) is one possibility. Do the words supplied for "Clouds" suit this painting? Many of them will. What other words could be used to describe the painting? Do these also describe Debussy's music? Many of these also will.

After this initial exposure students may be led to explore some of the compositional techniques Debussy uses to achieve his "impressions."

Second Listening

Debussy introduced a new way of thinking about melody and harmony. His scales were frequently pentatonic or whole tone.

Students are familiar with pentatonic scales from earlier study, but a review of these may be in order:

Procedure

Have the students sing these scales from the same starting pitch. After each, sing a song in that scale with text in *solfa*.

do-pentatonic	Rocky Mountain
re-pentatonic	Shady Grove
mi-pentatonic	(There is no English language folksong in this scale.)
so-pentatonic	I Gave My Love a Cherry
la-pentatonic	Land of the Silver Birch

Introduce the pentatonic theme used by Debussy in "Nuages":

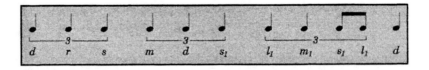

This is the "B" theme in what is a somewhat free A B A form.

Have the students sing and memorize this theme, then listen to identify its entrance and the instruments playing it as first, flute and harp, then strings, and then a return to flute and harp.

Third Listening

The students have sung and analyzed chord progressions in Mozart, Haydn, and Beethoven and they have also studied intervals. They should now be led to discover Debussy's unique use of intervals and harmonies. He was particularly fond of consecutive 5ths that seem to float in and out of key relationship. The opening theme of this piece is built of alternating 5ths and 3rds.

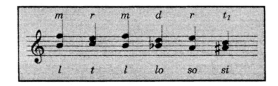

Have the students sing from notation first the upper voice, then the lower, and finally the two together. This theme could also be played on the piano, melalaphones, or xylophone in two parts. It should be performed sufficiently well as to be easily identified and recalled. It is played first by clarinets and bassoons and is followed by a short motive on English horn, answered by a two-note echo on French horn.

The English horn may be a new instrument to the students. If a live demonstration by a member of the symphony can be arranged this would be excellent. In the absence of such an opportunity pictures will suffice.

Similarities and differences to other woodwinds should be elicited with regards to size, material of which it is constructed and playing mode.

It's motive and the French horn answer may be sung:

Fourth Listening

Dynamics and tempo could be the focus of this experience. There is only one brief section in this piece with any marked dynamic contrast. It occurs about halfway through the piece as a gradual crescendo and diminuendo.

Tempo is slow and generally even with some ritardando at the end.

Using a Listening Chart

Perhaps it would be better with this piece not to chart it; to list the sections by form is to place an arbitrary shape probably not intended by Debussy. However, for the convenience of the teacher the following guide is offered. It could, of course, be given to the students at some point during the above lesson.

Work: Nuages from Nocturnes

Composer: Claude Debussy   **Dates: 1862–1918**

Style: Impressionistic

Section	Theme	Instruments	Dynamics
A	Cloud Theme	clarinets and bassoons	*mp*
	English horn motive	E. Horn, F. Horn	*mp*
	Cloud Theme	high strings	*mp-p-crescendo*
	English horn motive	E. Horn, F. Horn	*mp*
	Ascending passages	woodwinds	*crescendo*
	English horn motive	E. Horn, viola	*diminuendo*
	with viola counterpoint		
B	New Theme, pentatonic	flute and harp	*mf*
	Repeat of new theme	strings	*mf*
	Repeat of new theme	flute and harp	*mf*
A	Return to fragments of A theme	E. Horn, bassoons, cello	*diminuendo*

Conclusion

Students may draw comparisons with works of the Romantic period studied earlier. The contrasts are marked.

As a follow-up the teacher could play the second of these nocturnes, "Fêtes." It is a study in contrasts. Bright and lively it will dispel any notion that Impressionistic music is always soft and meandering.

LISTENING STRATEGY 15

Igor Stravinsky, The *Firebird*

1910 may mark the beginning of what we think of as twentieth-century compositional techniques. Compared to R. Murray Schaffer or John Cage or Ligeti, The *Firebird* of Igor Stravinsky is very mild and sonorous indeed.

But for its time it was a radical departure. While it built on the chromaticism of Debussy and the orchestration techniques of Rimsky-Korsakov it was nevertheless truly a product of the twentieth-century.

It could be a good beginning point into the exploration of music of the twentieth-century with students of any age because it contains standard twentieth-century compositional devices:

- bitonality
- chromaticism
- if not atonality, certainly some places where tonal center is hard to find
- mixed meters
- polyrhythms

Yet in among all this there are simple straightforward and very singable tunes in simple duple and triple meters with easy rhythms. Why?

- It's a fairy tale of sorts.
- There are evil characters represented by dissonant passages and by polyrhythmic and asymmetric meters.
- There is magic represented by a chromaticism without clearly defined tonal center.
- There are human beings represented by diatonic tunes in simple meters

The characters are right out of the folklore of all nations:

- There are princesses who have been captured by the evil king Kastchei (whose soul lies in an egg).
- There is, of course, the handsome prince.
- There is the good magic creature—in this instance a wonderful half bird/half woman who shimmers like fire and whose feathers hold wonderful powers.

This is an instance in which students' imaginations can be quite literally turned loose. Given the cast of characters and the music, what story will they create? How can they dramatize that story through movement?

However, before that can happen they must be familiar with the music. And before they can know the music they must be at a certain level of development musically.

They must know the chromatic scale in solfa. This was introduced in the course of studying the *Pastorale* Symphony of Beethoven, but should be reviewed now.

The students must also be able to deal with asymmetric and heterometric meters—this can be prepared by singing "Brother John" in $\frac{5}{4}$ and $\frac{7}{4}$.

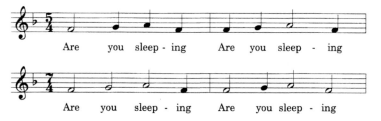

Are   you   sleep - ing   Are   you   sleep - ing

Are   you   sleep - ing   Are   you sleep - ing

Preparation for Listening

What musical skills and knowledge must students possess in order to listen to the *Firebird* Suite with enjoyment and understanding? The ability to:

- sing the complete chromatic scale.
- identify and perform asymmetric meters.
- identify and perform $\frac{3}{2}$ as a form of triple meter.
- distinguish between consonant and dissonant harmonies; diatonic and chromatic melodies.

Some of the above can be taught or reinforced in the context of the actual listening lessons. Other aspects should be prepared before listening.

Chromaticism

Students will have encountered, identified, and performed some chromatic pitches even in the music of Mozart and Haydn. At this point the complete chromatic scale may be introduced and hand-signs shown (or invented) for the pitches for which none officially exist. The ones shown on pages 184–185 were partially developed by teachers, added to or changed by students. The original Curwen signs did not contain chromatic notes.

Students should practice singing and signing the chromatic scale, as they have all the other scales they have learned.

First Listening

As an example of chromaticism in a melody they could listen to the opening of the ballet, with it's quiet, ominously chromatic theme setting the stage for magic, and then the appearance of the firebird in a setting of shimmering chromaticism.

1   "The Magic"

Second Listening

The circle dances of the princesses might be a good choice for the next stage of these lessons. It is an easily readable and singable melody, completely diatonic.

"THE PRINCESSES" THEME 1

"THE PRINCESSES" THEME 2

Students should read, sing, and memorize these two themes before hearing them. As they listen they can diagram the form and identify the instrumentation.

Some students could be encouraged to develop a dance pattern to be performed with this music. Later this dance could be inserted into a class enactment of the story they create to go with the music.

Third Listening

Play "King Kastchei's Dance."

Elicit responses from the class as to what might be happening with this supernatural evil character in the story at this point. *There is clearly conflict.*

How is conflict depicted in music? *Through dissonance.* Have students come to the keyboard to find examples of dissonance.

KING KASTCHEI'S DANCE

so

la

do

re

ti

do'

mi

fa

THE MOST COMMON CHROMATIC TONES

(so♯) si

(ti♭) ta

(do♯) di

(re♯) ri

At what point in the music is there a sudden change? Where do we suspect the human characters have reentered? *Where the music shifts suddenly to a quieter diatonic melody.*

Contrasting Theme

Fourth Listening

The next part of the ballet is entitled "Lullaby." What is a lullaby? How could it fit into our plot at this point? Is the melody diatonic or chromatic? (*Chromatic.*) To which of our characters could it belong? (*Only to the magical ones.*) How could sleep be used to solve the dilemma?

(fa♯) fi

The class should sing, memorize, and listen to this music.

Fifth Listening

The fairy tale is happily concluded and all rejoice:

Sing the theme until you know it well. Now listen. Something special happens to the meter at the end. Can you figure out what? (*It changes from* $\frac{3}{2}$ *to* $\frac{7}{4}$.)

Sixth Listening

When these five lessons have been completed the entire suite could be heard with students filling out a listening form.

Which theme?	What instruments	Rhythmic characteristics	Melodic or dissonant?	Magic or human characters	Chromatic or diatonic melody

Information for the Teacher

The story of the ballet, in brief, is that the evil King Kastchei has captured a bevy of princesses he holds as prisoners in a garden with a magic golden apple tree and a high fence.

The magical firebird attempts to steal the fruit, but is captured by Prince Ivan who is hunting. To gain her release, the firebird gives Ivan one of her magic feathers.

It is now nightfall and Ivan sees a beautiful princess who tells him of her captivity but warns him not to follow her, because the wicked king turns all who enter his garden into stone.

He nevertheless follows her. Alarms sound, and Ivan is surrounded by menacing creatures threatening to tear him apart. King Kastchei attempts to turn the prince into a stone, but the prince remembers that he holds the firebird's magic feather. He waves the feather and the Firebird instantly appears. Her magic is stronger than theirs and she compels Kastchei and his monsters to dance until they drop from exhaustion. The prince retrieves the egg that holds Kastchei's soul and breaks it—whereupon the spell is broken—Kastchei is no more and all he had bewitched awaken to joyous celebration, as the firebird bids farewell and flys away.

This is one of the most pictorially beautiful ballets of the twentieth-century. If a videotape (it has been filmed by the Royal Ballet) can be shown to the students at this point, it should be.

Ballet is not the easiest art form to introduce to teenagers. But if they know and can follow the story and are familiar with the music, students will enjoy it, and will, perhaps, approach their next experience in ballet with more open minds.

Chapter 9

Conclusion

The fifteen preceding Directed Listening Strategies are merely intended as models, not as finite curriculum choices. They are intended as an indication of the kinds of musical experiences students need if we are to produce musically educated adults.

Ideally each teacher should make his or her own choices as to the music through which to teach, keeping in mind the need for the inclusion of many periods and styles of music, many types of instrumental groupings, and many basic forms.

The listening strategies in this book have introduced music from every period from the Baroque to the early twentieth-century, have included symphonies and concertos, vocal music, keyboard music, and chamber music. Forms taught through these selections were fugue, minuet and trio, sonata, ritornello, passacaglia, through-composed and strophic songs, suite, theme and variations, and rondo.

It is hoped that teachers will augment and extend these sample plans with many based on selections of their own choosing.

The pattern for planning such long-range listening strategies is not a complex one; it may be applied to music of any period or style.

The choice of music is the most important facet of the design. Music should be selected because of its undeniable and enduring quality. That being said, it should simply be music the teacher loves, because that love of music is what will be communicated to students in every lesson. This aspect needs no plan, it will simply happen. If the teacher is enthusiastic about the work to be studied, that enthusiasm will be communicated to the students with every word and action.

Hungarian master teacher László Dobszay observed that there is a triangle effect among teacher, subject, and students: that if the teacher loves the subject and the students love the teacher, they will also love the subject.

Most of us have experienced one or more master teachers in our own lives who had the effect on us of making us love a subject we had not thought much about before. Choose music you love. It will be much easier to lead students to love it.

CREATING FURTHER LISTENING STRATEGIES

Once the music has been selected, several steps are necessary before introducing it to students.

- What is the background of this music? What pertinent information about period, composer, form, and instrumentation will add to students' enjoyment of this piece?
- What do students have to know before listening? What entry-level skills must they possess in order to approach the score in a literate and knowledgeable manner? What concepts should they bring to the study of this piece?
- What new concepts may be inferred through the study of this music? What new skills could be introduced or existing skills increased and refined through it?

At this point, by listening as often as necessary to the chosen piece, the teacher should construct and complete a chart form such as those given in the preceding chapters. This will help focus thinking on the aspects of the work—themes, form, instrumentation, tempo, timbre, texture, dynamics—most suitable for study. It will sharpen perception as to what has to be introduced, reviewed, or reinforced in preparation for listening.

Once this has been done, concrete planning can begin.

- List the entry-level knowledge and skills students bring to the work.
- List the new knowledge and skills required for an in-depth study of the chosen work.
- Decide which of these new learnings should precede a study of the work. Choose the musical materials for teaching these.
- Decide which of these new learnings should be taught through the work. Select the parts of the work through which to introduce them.
- Prepare the themes or motives for singing and memorizing. Notate them in singable keys for the students.
- Organize all the above material into a series of lessons, each focusing on a different aspect of the work.
- Include in your lesson cycle all the experiences through which students learn music: singing, playing instruments, moving, reading, notating, listening, and creating.

The Kodály Method has too long been solely the province of the primary grades in North America. While in Hungary it is viewed as the path to comprehensive musicianship, in most American classrooms it is thought of only as a way of introducing young children to music.

There is no doubt of its efficacy in the latter role, but not recognizing its potential value to higher levels of music education has led to generations of students not realizing their potential development in music.

ACHIEVING MUSICAL OUTCOMES

In Chapter 1 of this book the question is raised, "What should students be like at the end of twelve years of music education?" By way of an answer, ten outcomes of good music programs are stated in terms of student behaviors.

The student:

- *has achieved a high musical standard in performance.*
- *knowledgeably critiques performances, including his or her own, and makes or suggests desirable changes.*
- *has performed, listened to, and analyzed a wide variety of musical literature from all periods and styles.*
- *has developed vocal independence and a high level of vocal sight reading proficiency. He or she can both look at notation and think sound, and think or hear sound and notate it correctly.*
- *uses technical vocabulary correctly in analyzing and describing music.*
- *understands scientific principles of sound production and reproduction.*
- *understands the technical and theoretical aspects of music.*
- *is knowledgeable about the historical development of music.*
- *understands compositional techniques and is able on an amateur level to improvise and compose in a variety of styles.*
- *is able to discuss intelligently a variety of topics regarding music and musicians.*

The curriculum proposed in the preceding pages is designed to accomplish these ends. The student who has experienced the eighteen readiness lessons and either the fifteen directed listening strategies suggested or teacher-created ones similar to them will have the broad, solid base necessary for advanced music studies, or the appreciation and values that will make of him or her a knowledgeable audience member and active supporter of music in the community.

To play in the high school band or to sing in the chorus is not enough. Performance is important, but performance alone does not constitute an education in music. The time has come for music to take its place with the other academic disciplines as a subject worthy of serious study.

To that end this book is dedicated.

Bibliography

Music History and Listening

Barlow, Harold and Sam Morgenstern. *A Dictionary of Musical Themes*. Revised Edition. New York: Crown Publishers, Inc., 1975.

Bernstein, Leonard. *The Joy of Music*. New York: The New American Library, Inc., 1967.

Burkhart, Charles. *Anthology for Musical Analysis*. New York: Holt, Rinehart and Winston, Inc., 1972.

Copland, Aaron. *What to Listen for in Music*. New York: McGraw-Hill Book Company, Inc., 1957.

Grout, Donald J., and Claude V. Palisca. *A History of Western Music*. Fourth Edition. New York: W. W. Norton & Company, Inc., 1988.

Hitchcock, H. Wiley (ed.) *Twentieth-Century Music—An Introduction*. Third Edition. Englewood Cliffs: Prentice Hall, 1988.

Johnston, Richard (ed.). *Zoltán Kodály in North America*. Ontario: The Avondale Press, 1986.

Kamien, Roger. *Music, An Appreciation*. Fifth Edition. New York: McGraw-Hill, Inc., 1992.

Kamien, Roger (ed.). *The Norton Scores—An Antology for Listening, vol. 2*. Fifth Edition. New York: W. W. Norton & Company, Ltd., 1990.

Károlyi, Ottó. *Introducing Music*. Victoria: Penguin Books, 1965.

Kerman, Joseph, and Vivian Kerman. *Listen*. Second Edition. New York Worth Publishers, Inc., 1976.

Kerman, Joseph, and Kerman, Vivian. *Listen—Brief Edition*. New York: Worth Publishers Inc., 1987.

Machlis, Joseph. *The Enjoyment of Music*. Fourth Edition. New York: W. W. Norton & Company, Inc., 1977.

McGee, Timothy J. *The Music of Canada*. New York: W. W. Norton & Company, 1985.

Palisca, Claude V. *Baroque Music*. Second Edition. Englewood Cliffs. Prentice Hall, Inc., 1981.

Palmer, King. *Understanding and Enjoying Music*. Toronto: Coles Publishing Company Limited, 1978.

Roussel, Paul. *Mozart—Seen Through 50 Masterpieces*. Cambridge: Habitex Books, 1976 [translated by Ampersand Publishing Services Inc.].

Stolba, K. Marie. *The Development of Western Music—A History*. Dubuque: Wm. C. Brown Publishers, 1990.

Szabolcsi, Bence. *A History of Melody*. New York: St. Martin's Press, 1965 [translated by Jolly and Karig].

Young, Percy. *The Enjoyment of Music*. Manchester Square: EMI Publications, 1968.

Hungarian Sources

Bárdos, Lajos. *Selected Writings on Music*. Hungary: Editio Musica Budapest, 1984 [translated by Farkas & Ittzés].

Barkóczi, Ilona and Csaba Pléh. *Music Makes a Difference: The Effect of Kodály's Musical Training on the Psychological Development of Elementary School Children*. Hungary: Kodály Institute, 1982 [translated by Steiner and Pléh].

Dobszay, László. *After Kodály—Reflections on Music Education*. Kecskemét Zoltán Kodály Pedagogical Institute of Music, 1992. [translated by Ries].

Eösze, László. *Zoltán Kodály—His Life and Work*. London: Collet's Holdings Ltd., 1962. [translated by Farkas and Gulyás].

Eösze, László. *Zoltán Kodály—His Life in Pictures and Documents*. Hungary: Kossuth Printing House, 1982. [translation revised by Thompson].

Forrai, Katalin. *Music in Preschool*. Budapest: Franklin Printing House, 1988 [translated by Sinor].

Hegyi, Erzébet. *Solfege According to the Kodály-Concept*. Hungary: Zoltán Kodály Pedagogical Institute of Music, 1975 [translated by Macnicol].

Hegyi, Erzébet. *Solfege According to the Kodály Concept II*. Hungary: Editio Musica Budapest, 1979 [translated by Ittzés].

International Kodály Conference (conference proccedings) - Budapest, 1982. ed. by Bónis, Szönyi & Vikár. Budapest, Editio Musica, 1986.

Kodály, Zoltán. *Folk Music of Hungary*. New York: Praeger Publishers, 1971 [translation revised by Tempest and Jolly].

Sándor, Frigyes. *Musical Education in Hungary*. Second Edition. New York: Boosey & Hawkes Music Publishers Limited, 1969 [translation revised by Jolly].

Selected Writings of Zoltán Kodály. Toronto: Boosey & Hawkes Music Publishers Limited, 1974 [translated by Halápy and Macnicol].

Szönyi, Erzébet. *Musical Reading and Writing*. New York: Boosey & Hawkes Music Publishers Limited, 1978 [translation revised by Russell-Smith].

Vikár, László (ed.). *Reflections on Kodály*. Budapest: International Kodály Society, 1985.

Folksong Research & Collection

Canadian Folk Music—Books and Records. Calgary: The Canadian Folk Music Society, (1980). A pamphlet of suggested resources.

Cass-Beggs, Barbara. *Canadian Folk Songs for the Young*. Vancouver: Douglas & McIntyre Ltd., 1975.

Cass-Beggs, Rosemary. *The Penguin Book of Rounds.* New York: Penguin Books Ltd., 1982.

Chase, Richard. *American Folk Tales and Songs.* New York: Dover Publications, Inc., 1971.

Commins, Dorothy Berliner. *Lullabies of the World.* New York: Random House Inc., 1967.

Creighton, Helen. *A Life in Folklore.* Toronto: McGraw-Hill Ryerson Limited, 1975.

Curtis, Natalie (ed. & recorder). *The Indians' Book—Songs and Legends of the American Indians.* New York: Dover Publications, Inc., 1968.

De Turk, David A. and A. Poulin, Jr. (eds.). *The American Folk Scene—Dimensions of the Folksong Revival.* New York: Dell Publishing Co., Inc., 1967.

Erdei, Peter (ed.) and Katalin Komlos. 150 *American Folk Songs to Sing, Read and Play.* New York: Boosey & Hawkes, 1974.

Fowke, Edith (ed.). *Canadian Folk Songs.* England: Penguin Books Ltd., 1973.

Fowke, Edith and Richard Johnston. *Folk Songs of Canada—A Comprehensive Collection of Canadian Folk Songs.* Ontario: Waterloo Music Company, Ltd., 1954.

Fowke, Edith and Richard Johnston. *Folk Songs of Quebec (Chansons de Québec).* Ontario: Waterloo Music Company Ltd., 1957.

Gledhill, Christopher. *Folk Songs of Prince Edward Island.* New Brunswick: Centennial Print & Litho Ltd., 1973.

Hugill, Stan. *Songs of the Sea—The Tales and Tunes of Sailors and Sailing Ships.* New York: McGraw-Hill Book Company, 1977.

Hugill, Stan. *Shanties and Sailors' Songs.* New York: Frederick A. Praeger, 1969.

Johnston, Richard. *Folk Songs North America Sings.* Toronto: E. C. Kerby Ltd., 1984.

Jones, Bessie and Bess Lomax Hawes. *Step It Down—Games, Plays, Songs and Stories from the Afro-American Heritage.* New York: Harper & Row, 1972.

Korson, George (ed.). *Pennsylvania Songs and Legends.* Philadelphia: University of Pennsylvania Press, 1949.

Locke, Eleanor G. (ed). *Sail Away—155 American Folk Songs to Sing, Read and Play.* New York: Boosey & Hawkes, Inc., 1981.

Lomax, Alan. *The Penguin Book of American Folk Songs.* Baltimore: Penguin Books, 1964.

Lomax, Alan. *Folk Songs of North America.* New York: Doubleday & Company, Inc., 1975.

Manifold, J.S. *The Penguin Australian Song Book.* Australia: Penguin Books Australia Ltd., 1964.

Nettl, Bruno. *Folk and Traditional Music of the Western Continents.* Englewood Cliffs: Prentice-Hall, Inc., 1965.

Nettl, Bruno. *Folk Music in the United States - An Introduction.* Third Edition, revised by Helen Myers. Detroit: Wayne State University Press, 1976.

Newell, William Wells. *Games and Songs of American Children.* New York: Dover Publications, 1963.

Scott, Bill. *The Second Penguin Australian Songbook.* Australia: Penguin Books Australia Ltd., 1980.

Seeger, Ruth Crawford. *American Folk Songs for Children in Home, School and Nursery School.* New York: Doubleday & Company, Inc., 1948.

Sharp, Cecil J. and Maud Karpeles (collectors). *Eighty English Folk Songs from the Southern Appalachians,* ed. by Maud Darpeles. Cambridge: Faber Music Limited, 1968.

Songs and Stories of Canada. British Columbia: The Provincial Educational Media
   Centre, 1980.
Thomas, Philip J.. *Songs of the Pacific Northwest.* British Columbia: Hancock House
   Publishers Ltd., 1979.
Wositzky, Jan and Dobe Newton (eds.). *The Bushwackers Australian Song Book.*
   Australia: Anne O'Donovan Pty Ltd., 1978.

Discography

Johann Sebastian Bach
Toccata and Fugue in D minor, BWV 565

The *Pachelbel* Canon: The Canadian Brass Plays Great Baroque Music
Canadian Brass
RCA Red Seal RCD1-3554, 1983

Stokowski Transcriptions
The Philadelphia Orchestra
Wolfgang Sawallisch, conductor
EMI Classics 7243 5 55592 2 7, 1996

Baroque Organ Music
Hans-Jurgen Kaiser, organ
Deutsche Schallplatten DS 1056-2 [8:50], 1996

Johann Sebastian Bach
Brandenburg Concerto #5 in D minor, BWV 1050

Brandenburg Concertos
Tafelmusik Baroque Orchestra
Jeanne Lamon, musical director
Vivarte S2K 66289, 1994

Brandenburg Concertos
CBC Vancouver Orchestra
Mario Bernardi, conductor
CBC Enterprises SMCD5028-2, 1985

Brandenburg Concerto no. 4 in G major, BWV 1049; *Brandenburg* Concerto no. 5 in D major, BWV 1050; *Brandenburg* Concerto no. 6 in B-flat major, BWV 1051; Overture no. 3 in D major, BWV 1068
Slovak Chamber Orchestra

Bohdan Warchal, conductor
Madacy BC-2-3629 [22:09], 1994

Ludwig van Beethoven
Symphony #6 In F Major, Op. 68 (Pastoral)

The Complete Beethoven Symphonies
London Festival Orchestra; London Philharmonic Orchestra; Banburg
    Philharmonic Orchestra, Slovak Philharmonic; New Philharmonia
    Orchestra of London; London Festival Orchestra and Chorus; Lon-
    don Symphony Orchestra
Intersound CH1201, 1992

The Immortal Beethoven - Highlights of his most beloved music
Delos DE 1033
Recorded in Hollywood, California

Indiana University Symphony Orchestra
Thomas Baldner, conductor
Recorded at Indiana University, 1996

Ludwig van Beethoven
Piano Concerto #5 In E♭ Major, Op. 73 (Emperor)

Beethoven Concerto for Piano and Orchestra No. 5 in E-flat Major, Op. 73
Glenn Gould, piano with Toronto Symphony Orchestra
Karel Ančerl, conductor
Sony Classical SMK 52687, 1995

Anton Kuerti Plays Beethoven
Anton Kuerti, piano with Toronto Mendelssohn Choir; Toronto Sym-
    phony Orchestra
Andrew Davis, conductor
CBC records SMCD 5155, 1996

Kubelik Conducts Beethoven Piano Concerto No. 5, *"Emperor,"* Mozart
    Symphony No. 41, *Jupiter*
Clifford Curzon, piano with Bavarian Radio Symphony Orchestra
Rafael Kubelik, conductor
Originals SH800, 1994

Johannes Brahms
Symphony No. 4 in E minor, op. 98

The Brahms Collection, Volume 2
Philharmonic Symphony Orchestra
Frans Haas, conductor
Sony Music Special Products A 23159 [42:55], 1992

Symphony No. 4 in E minor, Op. 98
Royal Concertgebouw Orchestra

Riccardo Chailly, conductor
London 433 151-2, 1991

Symphony No. 4 in E minor, Op. 98, Variations on a theme by Haydn,
Op. 56a
Boston Symphony Orchestra
Bernard Haitink, conductor
CVP MS214, 1996

The Magic of Cello
Frederic Lodeon, Paul Tortelier, Xavier Gagnepain, Andre Navarra, Yvan
Chiffoleau, Roland Pidoux, violoncellos; Bournemouth Sinfonietta
Orchestra, Theodor Guschbauer, conductor; Ensemble Orchestral de
Paris, Jean-Pierre Wallez, conductor; Association des Concerts Robert
Lamoureux, Charles Munch, conductor
Erato 4509-94689-2, 1994

Joseph Haydn
Symphony no. 104 in D Major (Salomon)

Classics for Relaxation
Slovak Philharmonic Orchestra
Alfred Scholz, conductor
Mediaphon (distributed by Madacy Music Croups, Inc.) TTC-2-1714
[7:07], 1995

Consort of London with Haydon Clark
Collins Classics 1377-2, 1990

London Symphonies: nos. 103 & 104
La Petite Bande
Sigiswald Kuijken, conductor
Deutsche Harmonia Mundi 05472 77362 2, 1995

Wolfgang Amadeus Mozart
Horn Concerto #4 in E-flat major, K. 495

Works for Horn and Orchestra
Ab Koster, natural horn with Tafelmusik Baroque Orchestra
Bruno Weil, conductor
Vivarte SK 53369, 1993

Mozart Horn Concertos
James Sommerville, horn with CBC Vancouver Orchestra
Mario Bernardi, conductor
Disques SRC 1997 [16:51]
SMCD5172 CBC Records

Complete Mozart Wind Concerti
R.J. Kelley, horn with Orchestra of the Old Fairfield Academy
Thomas Crawford, conductor
MusicMasters 67180-2 [15:58], 1996

Wolfgang Amadeus Mozart
Symphony #41 in C Major, K. 5551 (Jupiter)

Ferenc Fricsay Conducts the RIAS Symphony Orchestra, Berlin
RIAS Symphony Orchestra, Berlin
Ferenc Fricsay, conductor
Decca DL 9745, 1995

Symphony No. 40 in G minor; Symphony No. 41 in C Major, *(Jupiter)*
Bohuslav Martinu Philharmonic
Peter Tiboris, conductor
Elysium GRK 710, 1996

A Mozart Festival
Camerata Academica; Berlin Orchestra; Mozart Festival Orchestra
Classical Heritage CH 1202-B, 1992

Wolfgang Amadeus Mozart
Serenade in G Major, K. 525 (Eine kleine Nachtmusik)

Overtures; Serenade no. 13 in G major, K. 525: *Eine kleine Nachtmusik*
Tafelmusik Baroque Orchestra
Bruno Weil, conductor
Vivarte SK 46695 [19:12], 1991

W.A. Mozart - *A Little Night Music*
Orchestre Pro Arte de Munich
Kurt Redel, conductor
Pierre Verany PV 730002 [19:13], 1994

Eine kleine Nachtmusik, K. 525; Serenade in D, K. 239 "Serenata not-
turna"; Divertimento in F, K. 247: Adagio; Notturno in D, K. 286; Ser-
enade in C minor, K. 388
Academy of St. Martin in the Fields; Heinz Holliger Wind Ensemble;
Iona Brown, Malcolm Latchem, violins; Stephen Shingles, viola, Ray-
mund Koster, double-bass
Sir Neville Marriner, conductor
Philips Classics 446 226-2, 1995

Franz Schubert
Die Forelle, D. 550

Fischer Dieskau with Gerald Moore in Concert
Deutsche Grammophon 431 085-2GH, 1985

The Schubert Album
Renee Fleming, soprano; Christoph Eschenbach, piano
London 455 294-2, 1997

Lieder
Bryn Terfel, baritone; Malcolm Martineau, piano
Deutsche Grammophon 445 294-2, 1994

Franz Schubert
Piano Quintet, op. 114, D. 667 "The Trout"

The Guarneri Quartett with Emanuel Ax
BMG 74321 24 202-2

Ax, Frank, Young, Ma, Meyer
Sony CD 61 964

Igor Stravinsky
The Firebird Suite

Stravinsky - The *Firebird*; Debussy - Nocturnes
Georgian Festival Orchestra, Tbilisi Festival Choir
Jahni Mardjani, conductor
Sony Music Entertainment QK66307, 1994

Stravinsky: "The Song of the Nightingale," The *Firebird* Suite, The
    Rite of Spring
The Minnesota Orchestra
Eiji Oue, conductor
Reference Recordings RR-70CD, 1996

Stravinsky the Composer
Philharmonia Orchestra
Robert Craft, conductor
MusicMasters Classics 01612-67177-2, 1997

Claude Debussy
Nuages

Nocturnes
Ulster Orchestra
Yan Pascal Tortelier, conductor
Chandos CHAN 8914 [7:25], 1991

Boulez at 70
Chicago Symphony Orchestra, Cleveland Orchestra, Vienna Philhar-
    monic Orchestra, Ensemble InterContemporain, Berlin Philharmonic
    Orchestra
Pierre Boulez, conductor
Deutsche Grammaphon GPL01, 1995

Debussy Images and Nocturnes:
Orchestre symphonique de Montreal
Charles Dutoit, conductor
London 425 502-2, 1990

George Frideric Handel
Water Music Suites - Suite No. 1 in F, Suite No. 2 in D, Suite No. 3 in G

Water Music
CBC Vancouver Orchestra
Mario Bernardi, conductor
CBC Enterprises SMCD 5032, 1985

Water Music
Tafelmusik Baroque Orchestra
Jeanne Lamon, musical director
Sony Classical SK 68257, 1996

Water Music
Academy of Ancient Music
Christopher Hogwood, conductor
Decca 443 177-2

Joseph Haydn
Cello Concerto in D Major, Op. 101

Cello Concertos
Anner Bylsma, cello with Tafelmusik Baroque Orchestra
Jean Lamon, conductor
Deutsche Harmonia Mundi 7757-2-RC, 1990

Haydn Cello Concertos
Ofra Harnoy, cello with Toronto Chamber Orchestra
Paul Robinson, conductor
RCA Victor Gold Seal 09026 70622 2, 1983

Music Index

Songs

Index

68 *Pastoral*, Fifth
Movement, 127
Symphony No. 6 in F Major,
Op. 68 *Pastoral*, 3rd
Movement (Allegro), 120
for Brahm's Symphony No. 4 in E
minor, Op. 90, 4th movement
(Passacaglia), 174
for Debussy's Nuages from
Nocturnes, 178
for Handel's *Water Music*, 158
for Haydn
Cello Concerto in D major,
Op. 101, 102
Symphony No. 104 in D
major, 116
for Mozart
Horn Concerto in Eb major,
K. 495, 97
Symphony No. 41 in C Major,
The *Jupiter*, K. 551, 108
Listening strategies. *See also* Directed
listening
constructing long-range, 78–79
creating further, 189–90
Liszt, Franz, 160
Literacy, musical, 73–74
Love of music, 2, 3, 188

M

Mahler, Gustav, 160
Major scales, singing, 41–42
Major seconds, 46–47, 50
Major thirds, 50, 90
Major triads, review of, 59–60
Masterworks, systematic study
of, 75–77
Melodic reading and writing,
beginning, 13–14
Melody
in Baroque period, 133
concept of, 25
diatonic, 180–81, 185
in minor to major, 138–39
minuet, 105

Romantic period, 160
Memorization, skill at, 12
Mendelssohn, Felix, 162
Messiah (Handel), 70, 152
Meter
in Classical period, 82
compound, 64–65, 68–69, 71, 88
concept of, 25
cut time in Bach's *Brandenburg
Concerto No. 5*, 144–46
in Handel's *Water Music*, 155–56
learned through repertory of
songs, 8
lessons on, 29, 31
review of, 34, 36–38, 66–67
simple, 64–65, 68–69, 71, 88
Minor seconds, 46–47, 50
Minor thirds, 50, 90
Minor triads, review of, 59–60
Minuet, 153
Minuet and trio form, 102–9
basic, 102–3
listening strategies for, 103–9
Mozart's *Eine Kleine
Nachtmusik*, K. 525, third
movement, *Allegretto*, 107–9
Mozart's Symphony No. 41, K.
551: third movement, 103–7
Mixolydian Mode, 120–22
Mode, change of, 138–41, 143
Modulation, 120
Monophony, rise of, 133
Mood in Baroque period, 133
Motives, 140, 141
Mount Royal Conservatory
lessons, 24, 28–72
Mozart, Wolfgang Amadeus, 76, 82,
83
Eine Kleine Nachtmusik, K. 525,
third movement,
Allegretto, 107–9
Horn Concerto No. 4 in Eb major,
K. 495, 86–98
Symphony No. 41, K. 551: third
movement, 103–7